White Sox Redemption

ALSO BY DAN HELPINGSTINE
AND FROM MCFARLAND

*The Cubs and the White Sox:
A Baseball Rivalry, 1900 to the Present* (2010)

White Sox Redemption
The Road to World Series Victory in 2005

Dan Helpingstine

McFarland & Company, Inc., Publishers
Jefferson, North Carolina

All photographs by Ron Vesely

LIBRARY OF CONGRESS CATALOGING-IN-PUBLICATION DATA

Names: Helpingstine, Dan author
Title: White Sox redemption : the road to World Series victory in 2005 / Dan Helpingstine.
Other titles: Road to World Series victory in 2005
Description: Jefferson, North Carolina : McFarland & Company, Inc., Publishers, 2025 | Includes bibliographical references and index.
Identifiers: LCCN 2025022845 | ISBN 9781476695839 print ∞
    ISBN 9781476655345 ebook
Subjects: LCSH: Chicago White Sox (Baseball team) | World Series (Baseball)—History—21st century | BISAC: SPORTS & RECREATION / Baseball / History
Classification: LCC GV875.C58 H47 2025 | DDC 796.357/640977311—dc23/eng/20250617
LC record available at https://lccn.loc.gov/2025022845

ISBN (print) 978-1-4766-9583-9
ISBN (ebook) 978-1-4766-5534-5

© 2025 Dan Helpingstine. All rights reserved

No part of this book may be reproduced or transmitted in any form or by any means, electronic or mechanical, including photocopying or recording, or by any information storage and retrieval system, without permission in writing from the publisher.

Front cover image: White Sox pitcher José Contreras delivers the first pitch of the 2005 World Series at U.S. Cellular Field on October 22, 2005 (photograph by Ron Vesely/*www.vesphoto.com*)

Printed in the United States of America

McFarland & Company, Inc., Publishers
  Box 611, Jefferson, North Carolina 28640
    www.mcfarlandpub.com

To
Max Allan Collins

Writer.
Mentor.
Friend.

Acknowledgments

There are always many people who assist a writer in a project like this.

First, I would like to thank McFarland for giving me the opportunity to publish this book, specifically senior editor Gary Mitchem, who supported me through some tough times which slowed the writing process. I will always be grateful to him.

I also appreciate the support and encouragement from Scott Reifert of the Chicago White Sox. His assistance was vital and important.

Every writer needs various types of feedback. Freelance editor Lucy Reynolds, with her work on the manuscript, improved the prose and made me a better writer.

The photos in the book, including on the cover, are from White Sox photographer Ron Vesely. Vesely has a knack for catching important historical moments. I am happy to include his images here.

I have received advice and information from Mark Liptak. Probably the only White Sox fan living in Idaho, Liptak is a top White Sox historian. Few compete with him regarding knowledge of the franchise.

I would also like to thank Mark Gonzales for taking time to talk to me about the 2005 White Sox. Gonzales covered the team for the *Chicago Tribune* and provided valuable insights.

And, finally, thanks to the 2005 Chicago White Sox. The team finally accomplished what most Chicago fans thought would never happen.

Table of Contents

Acknowledgments	vi
Introduction	1
Section One—Overcoming History	3
1. Curses	5
2. New Beginnings	13
3. Saying Good-Bye	24
4. Ushering in a New Stadium	35
5. Bo Knows Baseball	43
6. A New Way of Not Going to the World Series	51
7. Backlash	61
8. Overcoming Backlash	67
9. The Wells Season	76
10. Us vs. Them	80
11. Ozzie Guillén: Player and Then Manager	87

◆ ◆ ◆

Section Two—Making History	93
12. Exceeding Expectations	96
13. The American League in the Post-Season	106
14. One Last Stop to the World Series	117
15. Game Three: Anaheim	122
16. Game 4: Almost as If It Was Fixed—In a Different Way	124

Table of Contents

17. Game Five: On the Verge of Making History — 128
18. The Last World Series — 134
19. Houston Astros — 137

◆ ◆ ◆

Section Three—The World Series — 143
20. Game One — 145
21. Game Two — 150
22. Game Three — 156
23. Game Four — 160
24. Aftermath — 165
25. Decline — 174
26. Legacies — 178
27. Final — 187

Addendum: Roland Hemond, the Man Who Saved the Sox — 189
Chapter Notes — 197
Bibliography — 201
Index — 203

Introduction

As of this writing, it is 20 years since the Chicago White Sox won the World Series in 2005. That team certainly has not been forgotten, at least by White Sox fans. (However, at times, the team has been forgotten by ESPN.) Regardless, the actual memories are getting a little hazy with age, and many people probably don't realize what that team truly accomplished that year. It wasn't just that the White Sox won—it was *how* they won.

Of course, no player on the 2005 squad is now active in the Major Leagues. In addition, during the last part of the 101-loss 2023 season, bitter White Sox fans were despondent over a rebuilding program that hadn't produced the long-term winning that had been promised. Instead, they speculated about the possibility of their team losing 100 games for the second time in five years and were pessimistic about the long-term future of the franchise. All of this was happening during a time that was supposed to be part of the team's championship "window."

In considering the fans' discouragement and the fading memories of the winning 2005 team, I thought of two other significant winning years in Sox history: 1959 and 1983.

In 1999, for the 40th anniversary of the 1959 Sox team that won the American League pennant, the organization recognized the team. Players from the 1959 squad made their appearance at SoxFest, the annual winter-time fan event that hypes the upcoming season. Of course, it had been quite a while since that World Series, and aging players carefully made their way up a small ramp to stand in front of the fans.

As I applauded these past heroes, I realized I knew very little about the 1959 team. I was only six years old at the time of the

Introduction

Series and much too young even to realize what the World Series was. Except for Luis Aparicio, I had seen very few players from the 1959 team in person, and I had no real knowledge of what happened in the Series, which the White Sox lost to the Dodgers in six games. (Well, I knew a fan had accidentally spilled a beer on a White Sox outfielder trying to catch a home run, but that was about it.) As author Charles Billington wrote in his book *Comiskey Park's Last World Series*, "In spite of falling short of a world's championship, the 1959 White Sox remain indelibly etched in the memory of thousands of fans, justifiably filed away as their favorite baseball heroes."[1] Yet some of the younger fans at the 1999 SoxFest had never seen a game at old Comiskey or even seen the ballpark, which was razed soon after the 1990 season. By 2005, Comiskey Park and its last World Series participants were receding into history, as there was no physical reminder of the event.

In pre-game ceremonies before a Sunday afternoon game on September 17, 2023, against the Twins, the White Sox celebrated the 40th anniversary of clinching their first division title in 1983. Tony LaRussa, the manager, and outfielders Ron Kittle and Harold Baines walked out onto the field to throw out the ceremonial first pitch. The scoreboard jumbotron showed a replay of the winning run from the night of September 17, 1983. It was an ordinary-looking play with Baines hitting a sacrifice fly to drive in the winning run versus the Mariners. Julio Cruz scored the run with a leaping tag of home plate. But it wasn't an ordinary play. It was a key memory of a great White Sox team that just wouldn't make it to the World Series even though they won their division by 20 games. Regardless, many of the fans sitting in what is now known as Guaranteed Rate Field that day in 2023 were too young to know much about the 1983 squad in a direct sense, and the play had to look ordinary to them.

In 2025, another generation of White Sox fans is cheering their team on but has no first-hand knowledge or memory of the 2005 world champions. This book, in a small way, will address that problem. The 2005 team overcame history and other obstacles to win a rare White Sox World Series. That team, like the 1959 and 1983 teams, should be remembered. One key to the present is the past.

SECTION ONE

Overcoming History

The date was June 13, 1970. The White Sox were playing the Washington Senators. There was plenty of elbow room for fans that Saturday afternoon as only 8,281 fans were in attendance. White Sox pitching gave up five home runs among the 14 hits the Senators knocked around the park that game. The White Sox record dropped to 22–36 after a 12–7 loss. Things only worsened as the team ended up losing 106 games in one of the most awful seasons in franchise history. Twice in September, game attendance didn't top 700.

Nine years later, the decade ended in infamy. On July 12, 1979, the Disco Demolition promotion humiliated the White Sox in front of the whole country. In between games of a doubleheader against Detroit, disco records were blown up in a ceremony protesting the recent popularity of that music. So-called fans stormed the field and did so much damage to the field that the second game had to be forfeited to the Tigers.

White Sox fans, like others in major league cities, can do some odd things. These odd things have happened in both White Sox ballparks. But never, either before or after Disco Demolition, have the fans acted in this manner as a group. (The anti-disco movement had nothing to do with White Sox fans. It did have violent and racist factions. Many of the people who came to the park that night were not actually baseball fans. They certainly didn't act like it.)

Along with the memory of this humiliating spectacle, 1979 was the 20th anniversary of the last White Sox appearance in a World Series. Since the 1959 Series was the last and only such appearance since the 1919 Black Sox scandal, some fans felt as if the team had never been to the World Series. Or at least the younger fans who had never experienced such a thing.

Section One—Overcoming History

Fans were frustrated because owners John Allyn and Bill Veeck didn't have the resources to build a winning major league franchise. In the 1980s, any new ownership would have to have money. And they had to be willing to spend it. The waiting had gone on long enough.

1

♦ ♦ ♦

Curses

Curses. It is my opinion that curses exist only in the mind of the individual, yet many Cubs fans strongly believed that the "Curse of the Billy Goat" prevented their team from appearing in the World Series from 1946 through 2015. Finally, the Cubs went to and won the World Series in 2016, and the fascination with the billy goat ended, at least for the most part.

While curses are for the superstitious, Chicago baseball fans found it difficult to explain why their teams couldn't make it to the Fall Classic for periods that stretched into decades. Both the White Sox and the Cubs lost in such incredible ways that believing in a curse at least provided a rational explanation and prevented Chicago baseball fans from losing their minds.

September 27, 1967. Many White Sox fans of a certain and aging generation refer to this date as "Black Wednesday." After defeating Cleveland 3–1 on the September 24, the White Sox were in third place, a half-game behind second-place Boston, and one behind first-place Minnesota. The schedule was in favor of the White Sox as they played two games against the last-place Athletics in Kansas City and finished the season with three games at home against the eighth-place Washington Senators. Boston and Minnesota had to play each other, providing further help for the White Sox.

The first game against Kansas City was rained out, so a doubleheader was scheduled on the 27th. The White Sox would have their ace pitchers—Gary Peters and Joe Horlen—starting in the doubleheader. Things looked good as Peters and Horlen had won 35 games between them.

Section One—Overcoming History

Instead, things went bad and dark. The Athletics, who were on their way to Oakland and playing their last games in Kansas City, swept the doubleheader, 5–2 and 4–0, in front of 5,325 fans. At no time did the Sox have a lead in either game, and they picked up a grand total of seven hits. Now, to have any chance in the race, the Sox had to sweep the Senators back in Chicago. The only thing Kansas City did, even with the two wins, was solidify their spot in tenth and last place. (This was the second-to-last year before divisional play. The first-place team went directly to the World Series without a playoff.)

So, onward to play the Washington Senators at Comiskey Park. In the first inning, the Senators had men on first and second with one out. Right fielder Fred Valentine lifted a pop-up in foul territory off first base. Normally, the ball would have been caught, but the White Sox had installed a photographers well in anticipation of a World Series. First baseman Tom McCraw could not make the catch as the ball fell into the well, and Valentine had new life.

Valentine singled to left, driving in what proved to be the only run of the game. In the bottom of the ninth, the White Sox needed at least one run to stave off elimination. They had a foul out to the catcher sandwiched in between two strikeouts. In the end, the only time a batter made contact, he hit the ball backwards, and the White Sox were shut out for the second consecutive game. They had failed to score in 26 of their last 27 innings.

Afterward, during a locker room press conference, White Sox manager Eddie Stanky bolted from the room in tears. White Sox fans, frustrated and disappointed, cried, too, at least in a figurative sense. In a period of three days, the White Sox season had collapsed under the weight of a non-existent offense that managed only two runs against two bad teams. Although they finished only three games out, the Sox fell to fourth place. (As mentioned, the A's were already on their way to Oakland. Five years later, the Washington Senators moved and became the Texas Rangers. Thus, two ailing and losing teams combined to eliminate the White Sox from appearing in the World Series. Would White Sox history have changed if they had played St. Louis in the Fall Classic?)

1. Curses

Nineteen sixty-nine. All a person has to do is mention that year to a Cubs fan who lived during the 1960s, and that fan could be moved to cry also. You would have to have lived during 1969 to understand the mania that engulfed that team. Even Cubs players were awed by the hero worship and nonstop excitement at Wrigley Field.

From April 8—when Willie Smith hit a two-run homer in the bottom of the 11th inning to beat the Phillies in the Cubs' home opener—until September 10, the Cubs led the newly formed National League Eastern Division. They sent six players to the All-Star Game, and lefty Ken Holtzman threw a no-hitter against Atlanta on August 19 without a strikeout. Everything was going right, and Cubs fans were calling their team the greatest in the history of baseball. Players made outside money as records were cut and pizzas were sold. By August, one Chicago afternoon newspaper maintained an update on the magic number to clinch the division although it was a little early in the season to do that.

Then another Cubs curse. During the September 9 night game against the Mets in New York, a black cat walked past the Cubs' dugout. The little cat, which couldn't have weighed more than 10 pounds, terrified a group of grown men holding baseball bats. To no surprise, the Cubs lost that night and fell into second place the next day. They never regained first.

Of course, that frightened little cat had nothing to do with the Cubs' demise. But fans couldn't understand how their team had lost 16½ games in the standings to the Mets in the last six weeks of the season. What had first appeared to be a miracle and history-making season for the Cubs had turned into traumatic memories and emotional devastation. The Mets now became the miracle team and won the World Series title that Cubs fans had found so elusive since 1908.

Nineteen eighty-three. This time a Chicago baseball team would not be denied first place and a trip to the playoffs. Winning 99 games, the White Sox won the Western Division title with their closest rival nowhere near them. It was the first time either Chicago team had won a division title since divisional play began in 1969. Some

Section One—Overcoming History

observers said the White Sox rotation was so good, "it wasn't fair" to any opponent.

The White Sox trailed two games to one in the best-of-five series against Baltimore. (There were no wild cards at the time and just one playoff tier.) In Game 4, it was scoreless in the bottom of the seventh inning in Chicago. The Sox had Jerry Dybzinski on first base and Vance Law on second with one out. Julio Cruz lined a hard single to left. It was logical for Dybzinski to stop at second base since the ball was hit hard and the play was in front of him. But he headed toward third base even though Law had stopped there. "The Dibber" got caught in a rundown. Law tried to score and was thrown out at the plate in a play that wasn't close. The inning ended with no one scoring. The Dybzinski base-running gaffe had Sox fans scratching their heads then and for years to come even after Dybzinski explained himself to the media in a post-game interview.[1]

Tito Landrum homered for Baltimore into the left field upper deck in the top of the 10th inning for the game's first run. Baltimore added two more and won, 3–0. Thus, the once promising and possibly historic season was over. White Sox fans wondered why their powerful offense had scored but three runs in four games.

I discussed the 1983 team with outfielder Tom Paciorek some years later. Paciorek was sure that the White Sox had lost the day after they had clinched since the team had done so much celebrating. No, I told him, the White Sox won, 6–0, behind the complete-game pitching of Richard Dotson. Then Paciorek thought the Sox might have clinched too early and lost some of their edge. He recalled that A's right hander Mike Warren had no-hit the Sox a little less than two weeks after the clinching. That was true, but the Sox had won 11 of their last 14 games. I told the outfielder that his team had won 24 out of its last 30 games and outscored their opposition, 174–91, in that span.

"Wow," Paciorek said, "I never heard that statistic before." After some thought, he asked, "What happened?"[2]

White Sox fans who have painful memories of the 1983 playoffs are still asking the same question. The Dybzinski base running mistake wasn't the only explanation, and he shouldn't be scapegoated for

1. Curses

the playoff disappointment. But "what happened" still remains unexplained for many fans. The 1983 team had everything. Power. Speed. A great starting rotation. Good relief pitching. A solid defense, especially up the middle. Yet they didn't appear in the World Series. The whole thing traumatized fans and left behind nightmares instead of euphoric memories of a championship.

Nineteen eighty-four. It was an ominous year as the classic novel by George Orwell had predicted a dark and dank society. It was a year when the Cubs added to that feeling. Their fans probably imagined roaming around a cynical society where love was hate when another chance to go to the World Series was lost in a nightmarish vapor.

The Cubs had captured their first division title with 96 wins. Normally, they would have played three games at home in the best-of-five playoffs against San Diego, but at that time, Wrigley Field had no lights. Thus, it was decided that that last three weekend games would be played in San Diego, with two of them night games for better TV ratings.

At first, nothing, including the schedule, seemed to matter. The Cubs won both games in Chicago, 13–0 and 4–2. One win on the road would send the Cubs to the World Series for the first time since 1945. Seemed doable enough.

However, the Cubs lost Games 3 and 4 to tie the series. In Game 5, they took an early 3–0 lead on home runs by first baseman Leon Durham and catcher Jody Davis. Ace pitcher Rick Sutcliffe, who was 16–1 for the Cubs during the regular season, was on the mound. He had pitched seven two-hit, shutout innings in Game 1 and even hit a home run. Things looked good even with the Cubs having lost two in a row.

By the bottom of the seventh inning, the Padres had pulled within one. Carmelo Martínez stood on second base with one out. Pinch-hitter Tim Flannery sent a ground ball toward first baseman Durham normally an easy out. Martinez would advance to third, but there would be two outs.

Then disaster struck. The ball squirted through Durham's legs and into right field. Martínez scored the tying run. The Padres, an

Section One—Overcoming History

expansion team formed in the Cubs' failed year of 1969, added three more runs, won the game, and advanced to the World Series.

How did a dependable fielder like Durham make such an error at such a crucial time? Some said his glove had stiffened after sitting for a bit in Gatorade.[3] If that was the case, why had it been sitting in Gatorade? Regardless, the image of the ball scooting past Durham and into right field provided more nightmarish 1984 memories for Cubs fans that almost rivaled images of 1969 and the black cat.

Then came the Steve Bartman game on Tuesday night, October 14, 2003.

One more time, the Cubs led 3–0 in a game that could send them to the World Series. It was Game 6 of the NLCS against the Florida Marlins at Wrigley Field. Of course, Wrigley was packed. There was also a huge crowd on Waveland Avenue right outside of the left field bleachers. Cubs fans just wanted to be near Wrigley so they could be close to history. Little did that they know, a different kind of history would be made that night.

Eighth inning, one out, with Juan Pierre on second base for the Marlins. Left-handed batter Julio Castillo sent a foul down the left field line. Moisés Alou ran up to the wall, attempting to catch the fly. But a fan named Steve Bartman attempted to snag a souvenir and knocked the ball away from Alou. Alou threw a fit. The umpiring crew chose not to call fan interference as it appeared that the ball was over the stands, not in the field of play, when Bartman touched it.

Castillo walked, and things fell apart for the Cubs. The Marlins scored eight runs and won the game, 8–3. Cubs fans, including those on Waveland Avenue, chanted "asshole" at Bartman. Beer and food were thrown at him. Fans lunged at him as Wrigley Field security led him from his seat to the safety of stadium offices.

For so long, Cubs fans had had a Billy goat. They also had a black cat. Now they had Steve Bartman, a live and human scapegoat. As for thousands of Cubs fans, they humiliated themselves in front of the entire nation that night by lashing out at a fellow fan who had nothing to do with their team's collapse. It was simply another Chicago baseball collapse that couldn't be blamed on a curse.

Bartman went into hiding as the Cubs prepared for Game 7.

1. Curses

The Cubs took a 5–3 lead after pitcher Kerry Wood hit a three-run homer. But the Cubs could score only one run the rest of the way, and the Marlins won, 9–6. The Marlins were going to the World Series for the second time in six years, while the Cubs' World Series drought was extended to 58 years. The Marlins won the Series, their second Series win in those six years. The Cubs drought of not winning the Series was extended to 95.

Bartman remained in hiding, and to this day remains hidden, at least in a way. He has turned down numerous offers of money to make public appearances. In 2016, some Cubs fans wanted to apologize to him. He didn't acknowledge any apology or express a willingness to accept one. Since 2003, he still has made no public statement regarding the incident. With the exception of one reporter who attempted to secure an interview, only to fail, no one has seen Bartman in public, or at least, no one has said they have.

Two years later, another Chicago failure seemed to be on the horizon. The Cleveland Indians were making a run at the White Sox similar to the 1969 run the Mets had made at the Cubs. *Chicago Tribune* sportswriter Phil Rogers wrote a September 21 story chronicling the 1969 Cubs' heartbreak and other late-season collapses. Sox fans thought Rogers was hoping for a Sox failure. Many Sox fans, claiming bias by the parent company that owned the Cubs at that time, called the *Tribune* "The Cubune." Some felt Rogers wanted the White Sox to lose.

With the headline "It's Phils over Sox, '64 crash the worst," Rogers began his story this way: "The good news for Ozzie Guillén is he won't have overseen the worst collapse in history if the White Sox slide out of the playoffs. The bad news is that the one that followed Gene Mauch to his grave is the only one that would rank worse if this one eventually proves terminal." (Gene Mauch was the manager of the Phillies team that blew a 6½-game lead in the last 12 games.)[4]

In his book *Say It's So*, Rogers referred to the story as a *Tribune* article he wrote. He also referred to a Sox fan website, whitesoxinteractive.com, as having Sox fans who also thought the *Tribune* had a terrible bias against the Sox. He quoted White Sox center fielder Aaron Rowand as telling him the column "sucked."

Section One—Overcoming History

Was Rogers' story another form of a black cat? Would the White Sox, after having been in first place from day one, even get to the playoffs? Or would they find another Chicago way of breaking their fans' hearts by worrying about curses?

Instead, Cleveland would have their own Chicago-type sports nightmare. Center fielder Grady Sizemore, who would eventually win two Gold Gloves, lost a ball in the sun in the bottom of the ninth, and it popped out of his glove. The miscue let in the winning run in a loss to the Royals in a Sunday game in Kansas City. The Indians seemed to be psyched out by the play and subsequently lost five of their last six games. The White Sox clinched the division in Detroit a few days later.

History had seemed to be staring down the White Sox throughout 2005. Fans feared they were being toyed with and that more heartbreak was on the way. However, the White Sox would prove that things such as "Black Wednesday" and perceived curses were things fans worried about needlessly. The Sox became the fifth team in major league history to occupy first place from day one on and go on to win the World Series. In the playoffs, they first eliminated Boston, the defending world champions. They then beat the Angels, who had won the Series in 2002. They swept the Astros, who had a rotation including Roger Clemens, Andy Pettitte, and 20-game winner Roy Oswalt. The 2005 Chicago White Sox squad would prove to be the best in the history of the franchise. Curses and other bad luck be damned.

2

♦ ♦ ♦

New Beginnings

A financial group headed up by Jerry Reinsdorf and Eddie Einhorn completed its purchase of the Chicago White Sox from the Bill Veeck organization in late January 1981 for roughly $20 million. In general, White Sox fans welcomed the transaction because they were certain the new owners had to have more financial resources than Veeck. During the early days of free agency in the late 1970s, there was great player movement in Major League Baseball. However, big-name free agents were not making their way to the White Sox. This was illustrated by three straight losing seasons from 1978 through 1980. The only memorable event of these three seasons was a promotion that literally blew up in the team's face, leaving another menacing cloud hovering over the franchise.

From 1968 through 1980, the White Sox suffered through 10 losing seasons. This period began in 1968, when the team lost its first 10 games in a season when a World Series was expected. There were last-place finishes in 1970 and 1976. The team almost moved to Seattle after the 1975 season as financially strapped owner John Allyn looked for a buyer. For a time, there were no local takers until the Bill Veeck group purchased the team and kept it in Chicago. But in Veeck's five seasons of second-time ownership, only the 1977 South Side Hitmen had a winning record.

Reinsdorf and Einhorn realized they had to establish credibility with a frustrated, cynical, and impatient fan base. Any talk of building from the ground up would only stir anger. The new owners acquired Carlton Fisk and Greg Luzinski, two high-profile players with playoff and World Series experience. Who could forget Fisk's

Section One—Overcoming History

dramatic game-winning home run in the sixth game of the 1975 World Series that went off the foul pole at Fenway? And Luzinski? His size and power provided an imposing presence that historically White Sox teams rarely had. In the April 14, 1981, opener, 51,560 fans showed to see the White Sox pound the Brewers, 9–3. Fisk hit a grand slam, and Luzinski knocked in two runs. Hope was revived; credibility had been established.

On June 11, the White Sox sported a 31–22 record and were a mere 2½ games out of first place. There was a new optimism, and no one bothered to remember that the team had almost left Chicago a little less than six years earlier. But the season was interrupted by a two-month players' strike. Play resumed on August 10, but the White Sox played sub-.500 ball for the second half. In fact, during one game against New York, Yankees players openly laughed at the competition the Sox gave them. Suddenly, it looked like the bad old days again.

The next season, the team got off to a hot 8–0 start but cooled off quickly. By the 100-game mark, they were barely over .500. They went on to win a respectable 87 games but never came close to winning the division. With no wild card system, there was no chance for the playoffs.

White Sox fans allowed themselves to hope again in 1983. In the off-season, the team acquired free agent Floyd Bannister. The hard-throwing lefty led the American League in strikeouts in 1982 with 209. There is something sexy about a strikeout pitcher. In addition, the club had two promising rookies in Ron Kittle and Greg Walker. There were stories of Kittle's massive home run power in the minors as he hit 50 in 1982, and Walker had a beautiful-looking swing from the left side. Harold Baines was developing as a solid hitter, and there was the line drive-hitting Tom Paciorek, who had joined the team in 1982. The White Sox were not just Fisk and Luzinski. This team looked like true contenders.

At first, however, there was an air-deflating letdown. On May 26, the White Sox were only 16–24, seven games behind the defending division winner, the California Angels. On that day, Floyd Bannister was a disappointing and exasperating 2–6 as he lost to Texas. Bannister didn't pitch too badly that day as he gave up only three runs in

2. New Beginnings

7⅓ innings. But the Sox got only two hits and lost, 3–1. When a team isn't hitting, it looks lifeless. Suddenly, the season that had started with such hope looked like it would be another disappointment and a huge letdown.

By the All-Star break, the White Sox were within 3½ games of first-place Texas but were only three wins over .500. Their play had improved, but there still was little indication of the Chicago baseball history they would make.

On July 18, the White Sox were only two wins over .500, but they had climbed into first place in a weakened Western Division. It was a position they would not relinquish.

But even as it appeared that they had become the team to beat in the Western Division, Texas manager Doug Rader said he was not impressed. Or at least he felt that way from the scouting reports he said he was getting. The reports said the White Sox were "winning ugly."

White Sox fans were incensed. Their first-place team was being disrespected. "Winning Ugly" became the rallying cry. The new slogan was emblazoned on T-shirts. One banner hanging over the railing of the upper deck read: "White Sox—Love to Be Ugly." Fans gloated when the Sox travelled to Texas and beat the Rangers three out of four in late August. The Sox left the Lone Star state with a 68–54 record which was kind of pretty. The Rangers were in fourth place, 10 games out, and were never heard from again.

Then the Sox went to Kansas City for a three-game series. In game one, they faced lefty Paul Splittorff and won in a truly ugly way. Rader was vindicated somewhat, but the game only showed that the Sox were a special team.

Splittorff, who would win 166 games in his career, was a tough lefty. He was especially tough on the Sox in this game, but this was "Winning Ugly" White Sox. Splittorff would lose a game he should have won, and that he had won on so many occasions in his career, especially against the White Sox.

Greg Luzinski led off the second inning. Luzinski was the team's full-time DH and hit like one. During the "Winning Ugly" season, Luzinski made Comiskey Park history with three home runs over the

Section One—Overcoming History

stadium roof. Comiskey had a high upper deck, and reaching the roof rarely happened. In fact, from 1910 through 1982, only seven White Sox players hit homers over that roof.

In a way, Luzinski duplicated those roof shots by hitting a mammoth shot off Splittorff that cleared the left field bleachers. It seemed as if the ball went up in the air and was never seen again. In researching Kauffman Stadium history, the author did not find Luzinski's homer listed as one of the longest in the ballpark. Regardless, it was awe-inspiring as Luzinski got all of his massive arms into a perfect swing. The White Sox led, 1–0.

In the top of the third inning, Sox part-time outfielder Dave Stegman picked up a two-out single to left. The White Sox would not get another base runner until there were two outs in the eighth inning.

Inning after inning, Splittorff set the side down in order with the Sox not getting anything close to a hit. In the eighth, the score was tied at 1–1. It looked like all the Royals had to do was score one more run off Sox starter LaMarr Hoyt, and they would have a win. Splittorff was that dominant.

In the eighth, Scott Fletcher hit a routine, two-out ground ball to short stop U.L. Washington that should have ended the inning. The toothpick-chewing Washington was an excellent fielder who took care of just about everything hit his way. But this time, for some reason, he let the ball squirt out of his glove and roll away. It got just far enough that he had no play on Fletcher. Splittorff had retired 15 Sox hitters in a row and had made it look oh-so-easy.

Second baseman Julio Cruz was next. Cruz was a singles hitter and base stealer. With Cruz at the plate, it was reasonable to think the Sox would need two hits to score Fletcher because Cruz had two home runs for the season, and those homers had come back in the spring when Cruz played for Seattle.

But this was 1983, the year of Winning Ugly.

Cruz hit a deep fly to left-center field. Left fielder Leon Roberts and center fielder Pat Sheridan converged at the fence. Neither was able to make the catch as they helplessly watched the ball go over their heads. Cruz's drive, unlike Luzinski's tape-measure shot, was

2. New Beginnings

barely long enough. But it was a home run just the same and counted just as much—or counted a little more because it was a two-run shot, and the White Sox led, 3–1.

Splittorff tried to act stoic, but pain was all over his face. He set down the side in order again in the ninth, gave up three hits and one earned run in a complete game, and lost. The Royals, which had dominated the American League West and the White Sox during the late 1970s, were a little closer to elimination. While being interviewed on Chicago TV two weeks later, George Brett practically conceded the division to the Sox. The Winning Ugly White Sox were on their way to the first division title in Chicago since division play began in 1969.

The playoffs were much shorter and more intense back in 1983. Only division winners advanced to the postseason, and they played in a best-of-five series. A crowded pep rally at Daley Plaza in downtown Chicago sent the Sox to Baltimore to play the Eastern Division champion Orioles. Greg Luzinski led the cheers, shouting, "In four days, we're going to have a party and Rush Street will be dancing."[1] (Some would say leading the pep rally was not a good thing for Luzinski, although it's hard to understand that logic. Regardless, he would not have a good playoff series. In fact, he had a terrible one.)

The Orioles, winners of 98 games, would be tough opponents. The White Sox had won their title in a division that had no other teams over .500, and, in the end, had no real competition. Baltimore had had to beat back challenges from the Tigers and the Yankees. Were the Orioles the more prepared team?

White Sox fans hoped for a split in Baltimore. And they assured themselves of that with a 2–1 win in Game 1 on October 5. LaMarr Hoyt won as he held the Orioles to five hits. As he had in the game in Kansas City, Hoyt needed no closer as he went all the way. That's how it was for Hoyt in 1983. If he went into the ninth inning with any lead, the game was won. Now the White Sox were two games away from the World Series.

But then came Game 2.

Going to the ninth inning, the White Sox trailed 4–0. Baltimore starter Mike Boddicker had struck out 13 and held the Sox to four

Section One—Overcoming History

hits. But they were able to load the bases with two outs, bringing the tying run to the plate. A miracle rally perhaps?

Julio Cruz, the guy with the dramatic home run in Kansas City, was at the plate. With one strike, Cruz hit a line drive down the left field line that had extra bases written all over it. If fair, two, maybe even three runs would score, and it would be a real ball game. But the ball landed just foul. (Looking at a replay of the drive, I thought it was fair.) Cruz struck out on a high breaking ball on the next pitch, and the game was over. Baltimore 4, White Sox 0.

The White Sox had their split, but there was an uneasy feeling as the team headed back home. In Game 1, they had only scored two runs, with one unearned and the other coming home on a double play. Then they were dominated by a young pitcher who was in his first full season. If Cruz's drive had at least driven in a couple of runs, it would have helped from a momentum standpoint. But the Sox offense didn't look like a team that had scored 800 runs in the regular season, and they had been no-hit a couple of weeks before by Mike Warren of Oakland.

In the first inning of Game 3, things only worsened.

Game 3 was the first post-season game in Chicago since the World Series against the Dodgers in 1959. Excitement was high, and scalpers made money. Twenty-two-game winner Richard Dotson was on the mound for the Sox. Fans hoped for an exciting game. Instead, they got a disaster that paved the way for a huge heartbreak.

With men on first and second in the Baltimore first inning, Eddie Murray hit a three-run homer. It was no ordinary home run. The high drive went halfway up the right-center field upper deck. No doubt about it was the only way to describe the blast. Dotson didn't look like the 22-game winner of the regular season. He gave up another run in the second inning, and the Sox trailed, 4–0. Then came a series of events that helped turn almost all the series' momentum to Baltimore.

In the bottom of the fourth inning, with the score now 4–1, Mike Flanagen hit Ron Kittle in the knee with a pitch. As he hobbled toward first, Kittle yelled at Flanagen. Not only was the beaning painful, the White Sox felt the Orioles were throwing at their best

2. New Beginnings

hitters. In Game 2, Boddicker had hit Luzinski and Paciorek. Harold Baines then hit into a double play when second baseman Rich Dauer made a good play on the hard-hit grounder. Kittle left the game in the sixth inning. He would not play in Game 4 because of an injured knee and would be sorely missed.

Dotson, like many good starting pitchers, could get off to a rough beginning and then right himself. He had clean innings in the third and fourth. He got the first two hitters in the fifth. Al Bumbry hit a weak grounder to first, and Jim Dwyer hit an equally weak ground ball to second. From all appearances, Dotson had gotten into his groove. The score was still only 4–1, and the Sox still had a chance. Then Cal Ripken, Jr. stepped up to the plate.

Dotson hit him on the hip with a fast ball that didn't look all that fast. Ripken was far from hurt as the pitch barely hit him, and he even smiled before he took his walk to first base. The White Sox had sent their message, although Dotson had never been known as a headhunter. LaMarr Hoyt might hit you with a pitch and then smile at you. But not Dotson. Unfairly, the headhunter label stuck to him, although it didn't help that he later admitted he threw at Ripken.

Eddie Murray was next up. Dotson came inside, and Murray didn't appreciate it. He pointed his finger at Dotson and jabbered at him. Dotson returned the gesture, but he appeared flustered. He walked Murray on four pitches.

John Lowenstein walked up to the plate and worked the count to 2–0. Dotson had missed on seven straight pitches and was in danger of loading the bases. The aggressive Lowenstein, looking for something to drive, smacked a double against the right field wall, scoring Ripken and Murray. The score now stood at 6–1, and the game was all but over. Dotson defended his actions after the game. "They [the Orioles] only hit seven batters all year, and they hit three batters in one series," Dotson said. "Something had to be done. Pitching inside is part of the game."[2]

Regardless, getting into a beanball war backfired on the White Sox. It appeared that the Orioles shoved their aggressive play right back into their face and took control of the game and the series. The Sox let the game truly get away and lost, 11–1. Their fans were

Section One—Overcoming History

frustrated by the non-competitive performance in the first postseason game in Chicago in 24 years. Again, what happened to the offense? In three games, they had scored but three runs. The slumping White Sox were now on the edge of elimination.

The fall weather was dark, cold, and damp for the next game. The gloominess of the day matched the fans' outlook as suddenly the White Sox really looked ugly.

Lefty Britt Burns was slated to start Game 4. Burns was considered one of the brightest young pitchers in his first full season in 1980. He won 15 games for a sub-.500 team and had a 2.84 ERA. In 1983, he had a 10–11 record, but that was deceiving. He threw three shutouts and was durable. He beat the Indians in a complete-game five-hitter, 9–2, throwing 153 pitches.

In Game 4 of the American League Championship Series, the White Sox needed Britt Burns to pitch the game of his career. And he did just that.

But there seemed to be a hangover from the disastrous Game 3. In the bottom of the first inning, Carlton Fisk stood on first base with one out. Harold Baines hit a hard liner to Cal Ripken, Jr., who caught it about knee-high. He threw to first to double up Fisk, and the inning was over.

Was Fisk feeling any distraction from the controversy of the night before? Any runner had to make sure that liner got through the infield before getting too far off first base. With the ball hit that hard toward left field, it was not likely that Fisk could advance to third base in any case. So the inning ended, with your cleanup hitter leading off the second inning with no one on base. Was Fisk truly distracted? No one can know, but this was not a play a veteran would normally have made, especially a veteran with World Series experience, and it killed the inning. It was also an indication of things to come. If Baines' drive had somehow gotten through for a single, the Sox would have had a chance for an early lead. Instead, they went to get their gloves and went back onto the field after putting up another scoreless inning.

Meanwhile, Burns' fastball was lively, his breaking stuff kept Baltimore off-balance, and he held them scoreless into the seventh

2. New Beginnings

inning. The problem was that the Sox offense continued to struggle, and the game remained a scoreless tie. In the bottom of the seventh, a base running gaffe ruined a chance for the Sox to break the game open, or at the very least take the lead.

Greg Walker started things with a single, and manager Tony LaRussa sent in Mike Squires to run for him. Vance Law singled to left, and Squires stopped at second. The light-hitting Jerry Dybzinski tried to bunt the runners to second and third, but Orioles catcher Rich Dempsey threw to third to force Squires. Julio Cruz lined a single to left. The way the ball was hit, and with the outfield playing shallow for a singles hitter, there was no way Vance Law could score. Law stopped at third. It looked like the Sox would have the bases loaded with one out. Then some weirdness happened.

For some odd reason, Dybzinski continued onto an occupied third base. He was caught in a rundown. Vance Law, hoping the Baltimore defense would be distracted by Dybzinski, headed for home. Todd Cruz ignored Dybzinski, fired home to Dempsey, and Law was out by about 10 feet. The Sox went from bases loaded and one out to first and second with two outs. The cheers that had followed the Cruz hit went silent as fans wondered what in the hell had just happened.

Left-hander Tippy Martinez was on the hill for the Orioles, and he balked the runners to second and third. A hit could score two runs, but left-handed Rudy Law was having a hard time with Martinez, which is not uncommon in a lefty-lefty match up. Law hit a soft fly to left to end the inning and the threat.

Baltimore loaded the bases with two outs in the eighth inning, but Burns got pinch-hitter Dan Ford to pop out to Julio Cruz in short right. Burns still had a shutout.

In the Baltimore ninth, the Orioles went three-up, three-down. The line on Burns for nine innings was 142 pitches, no runs, five hits, five walks, and seven strikeouts. All the White Sox needed was a run in the ninth, and they would force a fifth and deciding game. For a moment, it looked like they would do just that.

With two outs, Dybzinski redeemed himself some with a single to left. He advanced to third base on a single by Julio Cruz, Cruz's third hit of the day. Rudy Law was next, and any kind of hit would

Section One—Overcoming History

win the game. Or a wild pitch. Or a passed ball. Or an error by the Baltimore defense. Almost anything. Wouldn't it be something if Jerry Dybzinski scored the winning run? Then his baserunning mistake would mean nothing.

Law worked the count full. A walk would be good, too. Carlton Fisk was in the on-deck circle. The crowd waited, hoping for something big, waiting to let out a roar of a cheer. Law took strike three. Apparently, he still wasn't picking up Martinez well. The crowd sat back on its hands as the game moved on to the 10th inning. Sitting in the right-center field seats, I was amazed that Law took a third strike with the season on the line.

Burns remained in the game and struck out John Shelby to start the 10th. Tito Landrum was next. Landrum had played in 32 games in the 1983 season and had one homer. He doubled his home run count by breaking the scoreless tie with a homer off Burns.

It was no cheapie. Landrum had taken a big cut and sent a high drive through the cold, fall wind. The ball landed in about the third row of the upper deck, the second upper deck home run for the Orioles in as many days. Burns left the game after 9⅓ innings. Baltimore added two more runs to put the game out of reach. The series was over. The season was over.

Comiskey Park sat in stunned silence after Tom Paciorek struck out for the last out. In four games, the Sox scored three runs and were shut out twice. During the regular season, there had been rooftop homers and great moments. After Game 1 of the playoffs, however, there were big disappointments and embarrassments. The Sox hit no homers in the series, rooftop or otherwise.

This loss certainly was not a matter of bad luck or a curse or a possibly evil black cat. Baltimore simply made the plays it had to make.

In the third inning, with Julio Cruz on second, Rudy Law hit a deep fly to right and Landrum made a nice running catch on the warning track. The next inning left fielder Gary Roenicke made a diving grab of a Harold Baines drive that would have been at least a double. Leading off the eighth, Fisk hit a fly to the deepest part of the ball in right center, but John Shelby snared it just before he got to the wall.

2. New Beginnings

And the Rudy Law strikeout in the ninth? From my seat in right-center, I couldn't see the pitch. All I saw was the umpire's right arm going up emphatically. Years later, I saw the pitch clearly as I watched the Jeff Einhorn documentary on the Winning Ugly season. Tippy Martinez threw a breaking pitch right under Law's hands and tied him up. Law may have been looking for a fastball on a 3–2 pitch, but Martinez risked loading the bases and made a great pitch. Anything else and the White Sox probably would have won it in the ninth. For a fifth game, eventual Cy Young Award winner Hoyt would have been back on the mound. The World Series would have been within grasp.

But there was no fifth game because the Orioles played like a championship team that day. They continued that type of play in the World Series and beat the Phillies in five games. As for the Sox, the headline on the *Chicago Sun Times*' page one the next day said it all with the bold letters reading, "It Was the Ugliest Day of the Year." A photo of a disconsolate Britt Burns standing on the mound after the Landrum home run took up a large space and said more than the headline.

And Britt Burns? Orioles players had stood on the steps of their dugout when he was taken out by Tony LaRussa and gave him an ovation for a pitching performance that should have led his team to play at least one more day. The fans stood for him, too. Years later, I interviewed Burns for another book. I asked him if he had any qualms about the pitch he threw Landrum. He looked at me strangely, and I realized why. My question was a dumb one. He gave his team every chance to win an important game by pitching nine shutout innings. Unfortunately for Burns and the White Sox, his team had been beaten by a better opponent, an opponent that made every play it needed to make.

The Orioles showed class with their respectful ovation for Burns. Baseball history should give him one, too. He gave a clutch performance that has been matched by only one other White Sox pitcher in that type of situation, and that happened 25 years later. He had pitched the game of his life and lost. The Sox World Series was still 22 years away.

3

♦ ♦ ♦

Saying Good-Bye

Nineteen ninety was the last baseball season for old Comiskey Park. The stadium, which opened on July 1, 1910, was considered state of the art in its early days. Unlike earlier major league counterparts, it was not a wooden firetrap. However, fans would get frustrated by the rising steel girders of the lower deck as they sometimes blocked vision. Some seats were next to the girders, forcing fans to look around the structure.

Wrigley Field has always been described as beautiful, but Comiskey Park looked majestic at night, with the massive lights reflecting off the deep green outfield grass. Comiskey was a large, expansive stadium. It was definitely a pitcher's ballpark with dimensions of 353 feet down the lines, 375 in the power alleys, and 415 to dead center. Bill Melton used to kid Ron Santo when the former Cubs third baseman came to play for the Sox in 1974. Melton told Santo that some of those home runs he hit at Wrigley would have been outs in Comiskey.

Ultimately, the size of the park became a problem. Even when the White Sox were winning, they hit few home runs and relied on their pitching staff for success. Manager Eddie Stanky had to defend his club in 1967. The White Sox were in an exciting pennant race that year with four teams contending until the last weekend of the season. Yet, Stanky had to fight back accusations that his team was dull and almost unwatchable. "We're last in homers, we're last in hitting, and last in war and peace. But we're first in guts and determination."[1]

On the day Stanky stuck up for his club, the Sox were shut out by the Yankees' Bill Monbouquette, 5–0. The Sox got five hits that

3. Saying Good-Bye

day, four in the infield. A quiet and small crowd of 11,475 sat on its hands most of the game as the Sox offense showed little life. Even their pop-ups looked pathetic.

Things came to a head after the 1968 season. The White Sox hit only 71 homers that year. In addition, their all-pitching-no hit formula no longer worked. Eddie Stanky was fired at mid-season. Their consecutive streak of winning seasons that began in 1951 came to a halt as the Sox lost 95 games. Baseball as a whole suffered as pitchers dominated in 1968. The American League had only one .300 hitter who qualified for the batting title, and Carl Yastrzemski took the title with a .301 average. Boring, low-scoring games were the norm, and the White Sox had more than their share. Team attendance sank.

Owner Arthur Allyn had a partial solution. He decided to make the ballpark more hitter-friendly and, hopefully, generate at least some offense. One part of the solution was to install Astroturf in the infield. The intent was to speed up ground balls in the hope of getting them into the outfield for singles and maybe doubles.

Solution number two was to shorten dimensions to produce more homers. With the changes, it was now 335 feet down the lines, 370 in the power alleys, and 400 in dead center.

The White Sox did hit a few more home runs in 1969, but so did their opposition. For the second season in a row, the team lost over 90 games. Attendance sank even further. It didn't help that the Cubs had their exciting year in 1969, and baseball attention in Chicago shifted to the North.

There were other problems with the stadium modifications. The Astroturf covered the infield only, and the stadium lost some of its beauty as the infield resembled a pool table. Instead of moving the plate out to shorten the dimensions, the team erected short, green, cyclone fences in front of the old walls. In addition to cheapening the stadium's appearance, some home runs fell in between the new fence and the old wall. Fans knew those homers would have been outs before the modifications were made. It was hard to get excited about that.

The White Sox also hit a few more homers in 1970, but the team had another losing season, in fact one of their worst. Attendance

Section One—Overcoming History

further declined to embarrassing levels. Ownership came to its senses and took down the Little League–looking fences. Left and right field dimensions were restored, although center field remained at 400 feet.

The Astroturf stayed, even though there was no proof that it produced more offense. If anything, it helped infield defense as ground balls had a truer bounce. Bill Veeck tore out the Astroturf at the beginning of the 1976 season. Comiskey Park, with its arched windows, looked like a major league ballpark again.

Upon taking over the team in 1981, Jerry Reinsdorf insisted that the franchise needed a new stadium if it was going to compete on the major league level. Baseball economics was changing. Once, fans who went to three to five games a year were important. Now, not so much. The corporate fan was considered more vital. A new stadium would have sky boxes and other corporate amenities.

In addition, the obvious fact was that the stadium was old. The new ownership stated that it was in terrible shape, and refurbishing it was not practical. Comiskey had to be replaced. Not only would the park be replaced, it would be razed, and the new stadium would be built across the street.

For many long-time fans, losing Comiskey Park would be painful. They would no longer be able to sit in the stadium that held so many memories. The fact that Jerry Reinsdorf used a possible move to St. Petersburg, Florida, as leverage to get public funding for the new ballpark didn't make him popular.

White Sox fans faced the beginning of the 1990 season with sadness and dread. Their beloved stadium was in its last year of use. Also, their team had just suffered through four straight losing seasons during a rebuilding stretch. Like an old 45 vinyl record, the 1983 division title seemed like it happened in a different era.

Slightly over 40,000 fans attended the last Opening Day at Comiskey Park. The White Sox scored two runs. One came on a wild pitch. One scored on a sacrifice fly. The White Sox got only one RBI for the day. Yet they won, beating the Brewers, 2–1.

To the surprise of many fans, the White Sox kept winning. Many times, they won in the same manner. On Sunday, May 13, the Sox

3. Saying Good-Bye

were playing the last game of a three-game set against Kansas City. They had won the first two games and took a 2–1 lead in the second inning of the third game. They scored two runs with the benefit of only one hit—something like the 2005 team.

Then the Sox offense went silent. The Royals picked up a run in the sixth inning on a homer to right field by Gerald Perry. KC went ahead with a run in the seventh. By then, although the Royals were ahead by only one run, it seemed as if they had the game in hand. The Sox offense just wasn't generating anything.

But the White Sox tied it in the eighth, doing it the 2005 way once more. Lance Johnson singled, stole second, and came home on a Dan Pasqua single.

In the top of the ninth, the Royals had a chance to break the game open when they loaded the bases with one out. They had Bo Jackson and George Brett coming up. But Jackson struck out, and Brett hit a routine grounder to shortstop Ozzie Guillén. Threat over. Game still tied.

Scott Fletcher led off the bottom of the ninth with a double and advanced to third when Jackson misplayed the ball in left-center. Royals manager John Wathan ordered the next two hitters walked to set up a force play at the plate.

Lance Johnson hit a medium fly to left fielder Jim Eisenreich. Eisenreich's throw home got there on the fifth bounce. Fletcher barely beat it, but he scored. The White Sox won, 4–3.

I was sitting on the first base side, so I was able to get a good look at the Royals as they left the field. They all wore stunned expressions, as if they didn't know how this White Sox team had beaten them that day and on three straight days. The White Sox had spent the last half of the 1980s losing. The White Sox now had a 17–10 record. This White Sox team was only two games out of first.

By the time the first-place and defending world champion Oakland A's came to Chicago for a weekend four-game series on June 14, the White Sox were 36–20 and still two games out of first place. These were the A's of Mark McGwire and José Canseco. These were the A's that won 104 games in 1988 and 99 in 1989. The arrogant A's. Pitcher Dave Stewart was not impressed by the second-place White Sox.

Section One—Overcoming History

"They seem to think they have some pretty good players," Stewart said. "There aren't many players over there who could hold my jock as far as I'm concerned."[2]

The arrogant A's left Chicago winning three of four games, the last one 12–3. The Sox were now four games out, and it seemed like a very distant four games.

A week later, the Sox travelled to Oakland for a three-game set. And what did the little White Sox do? They swept the series.

In game three, Chicago edged Oakland, 3–2, in 10 innings in front of 44,347 fans. Yes, Oakland drew over 40,000 for a game. In fact, they drew over 40,000 for all three games and garnered about 130,000 spectators for the series. In the last game, Dan Pasqua homered off Dave Stewart in the 10th inning. Yes, pitchers threw more than six innings in those days. Stewart would throw 11 complete games that year.

At the end of the series, the White Sox left Oakland one game out, one game behind the arrogant A's. During the series in Chicago, Sox fans didn't appreciate Stewart's jockstrap remark. In response, someone had taken a huge white cloth and cut it up to make it look like a jockstrap. They put Stewart's name on the top in black lettering and hung it over the railing of the left field upper deck. He could try it on if he wanted.[3]

July 1, 1990, marked the 80th anniversary of the opening of Comiskey Park as the White Sox played the Yankees. The stadium had held its first game on July 1, 1910, when the White Sox hosted the St. Louis Browns. St. Louis won the game, 2–0, behind the complete-game pitching of Barney Pelty. Ed Walsh was the bad-luck pitcher for the White Sox. Two years earlier, Walsh had won 40 games and logged 464 innings. Walsh was elected to the Hall of Fame in 1946. The St. Louis Browns moved to Baltimore and became the Orioles in 1954.

In the July 1, 1990 game, a different type of history was made.

As in the 1910 game, there was a real pitcher's duel. Promising young left-hander Greg Hibbard was on the mound for the White Sox. Andy Hawkins pitched for New York. Hawkins was only 1–5 coming into the game, but he had had some excellent years in San

3. Saying Good-Bye

Diego which included an 18-win season in 1985. In 1989, he won 15 games.

Both pitchers threw no-hit ball for the first five innings. Combined, they got the first 29 batters out in succession. The double perfect game ended with two outs in the bottom of the fifth inning when Hawkins walked Ron Karkovice.

Hibbard gave up two hits in each of the sixth and seventh innings but gave up no runs. He left after the seventh and got a no-decision for his shutout efforts.

But Hawkins remained in the game and still had a no-hitter in the eighth. After he got the first two hitters in that inning, things went very wrong for Andy Hawkins.

Sammy Sosa hit a sharp grounder to third. It was not an easy play for third baseman Mike Blowers as he had to backhand the ball. However, he didn't have to move much, and it was a play a major leaguer could and should have made. Blowers bobbled the ball at his feet. He recovered quickly and fired to first. Sosa beat the throw with a headfirst slide.

The scoreboard operator registered the play as a hit. The Yankees' bench fumed as they glared up at the press box. It turned out the official scorer was calling the play an error, and the scoreboard operator had made an error of his own. "I called it right away," official scorer Bob Rosenberg would say. "The Yankees in the dugout were giving me the finger."[4]

So the no-hitter was still intact. (In reality, no scorer would have called that a hit in that situation.) Ozzie Guillén was next, and Sosa stole second with another headfirst slide. Guillén walked.

Lance Johnson was the next hitter, and he walked on four pitches. Yankees manager Stump Merrill came out to talk to Hawkins. Merrill was in a bind because he wanted Hawkins to have a shot at his no-hitter, but Hawkins seemed to have lost his command. The Yankees had two relievers warming up in the bullpen, but they didn't appear ready, so Merrill left Hawkins in for at least one more hitter, with the hope that another walk wasn't on the way.

Robin Ventura was up and showed some good hitting technique by going with an outside pitch to left. However, Ventura hadn't hit

Section One—Overcoming History

the ball all that hard. Left fielder Jim Leyritz went to his left when he should have started to his right, but he was able to correct his route. He was not directly underneath the rather routine fly ball, but he was still in position to make the catch, yet he muffed it. The ball glanced off the edge of his glove and rolled to the wall. It was the second Yankees error of the inning, and it was costly. With two outs, the runners were on the move, and the bases were cleared easily. The Sox led, 3–0, and Ventura stood on second base.

Iván Calderón came to the plate. He, too, went to the opposite field with another routine fly. The Yankees had been battling the sun all afternoon, so right fielder Jesse Barfield played the ball off to his side. Bad move. The ball also went off the edge of his glove, and Ventura scored the fourth run of the inning.

Dan Pasqua popped to short to end the inning. Not playing anything off to the side, shortstop Alvaro Espinoza made the catch in an emphatic way, showing his frustration. In the inning, there were three errors, two walks, and four unearned runs. And all of it happened after two were out. But Andy Hawkins still had his no-hitter.

The Yankees went down quietly in the ninth, and the White Sox had their strange win. Reliever Barry Jones got the win because he pitched a clean eighth inning. Conversely, Andy Hawkins got the loss because his eighth inning hadn't been so clean.

It was fitting for Sox fans that the Yankees were the losers in this odd game. Through the decades, the Yankees had come to Comiskey Park with players like Ruth, Gehrig, DiMaggio, Mantle, Maris, Berra, and Ford, and they had beaten the Sox with regularity. At the end of the day on July 1, 1990, however, the Yankees sat in last place in the AL East. The White Sox were in first place, percentage points ahead of the arrogant Oakland A's.

Yet the win wasn't as fluky as it may have appeared. The White Sox got a solid effort from their starter, and the bullpen gave up no hits in the last two innings. Fluky game or not, the Yankees were never in the position to win. The White Sox—the no-hit White Sox—were the better team, as they often were in 1990.

The White Sox went into Oakland on September 17 with an 84-62 record, 22 wins over .500. However, the arrogant A's were

3. Saying Good-Bye

having another one of their dominant years and had a 10-game lead over the Sox. Oakland would finish the season with 103 wins.

The White Sox won the first two games in impressive fashion, 7–0 and 8–2, as part of a six-game winning streak. Nasty Dave Stewart helped the A's avoid another sweep by winning game three, 7–3. It was his 21st win of the season. He even had some good words for the White Sox. "That ballclub has a lot to be proud of," Stewart said. "They've got a lot to hold their heads up about."[5]

The White Sox *did* have a lot to be proud of even if the Western Division title was out of reach. They beat the arrogant A's in the season series, 8–5. As for the A's, they weren't so arrogant after the World Series. The Reds swept them in four games.

This will date me terribly, but I attended my first game at Comiskey Park on Friday, August 12, 1960. Strangely, it was a day game because usually Fridays were night games. The opposition was the Kansas City A's, who were sometimes known as the farm club for the New York Yankees. There were 8,439 fans in attendance.

Naturally at that age, I was awed by the huge stadium. In the eighth inning, A's left fielder Norm Siebern homered. I never saw it. The crowd stood to get a better look at the drive. I stood, too, well, because everyone else had stood. The only thing I saw was people's backs.

The White Sox won the game, 6–4, on the strength of a six-run sixth inning. At the end of the day, the Sox were only a half-game behind the first-place Yankees. But Chicago would not repeat as pennant winners. They finished 10 games behind the Yankees, who would play an historic World Series against the Pittsburgh Pirates.

Of course, all of this was long before the advent of social media and the sophisticated way of purchasing tickets. For a time during the 1960s, the White Sox had small, house-like structures situated right outside the stadium. Ticket sellers sat in the structures, and each had a sign right above it. If a fan wanted seats down the third base line, he'd go to the structure marked "Third Base Line," and so on. There was something charming about this.

At one time, the organ was a large part of the entertainment at the park. In 1970, the White Sox hired Nancy Faust. She would

Section One—Overcoming History

become more beloved to Sox fans as time went on. When she retired, she stood in short center field to say goodbye. The line of fans went around the stadium concourse.

A shower provided a memorable image of Comiskey Park, although it wasn't a traditional shower, and it also became a symbol of an unexpectedly exciting season.

If a fan didn't mind getting their clothes wet, they could cool off the old-fashioned way by stepping under an open shower installed in the center field bleachers. A constant image of the 1977 South Side Hitmen season was the stream of water flowing down from a round shower head. As the Hitmen slugged the ball all over Comiskey, fans doused themselves. The shower was another Bill Veeck idea to address simple needs. Plenty of fans took advantage of it as they soaked in the aura of one of only two winning seasons during the 1970s.

These were the types of memories the almost 43,000 brought with them when they attended the last game at Comiskey Park on September 30, 1990. The White Sox won the game in typical 1990 fashion, 2–1, an ending fans could remember warmly.

But even with that bit of happiness, the win was not the most important thing that day. As the players left the field, fans fully realized old Comiskey was going to be torn down. The new park already loomed in the background, looking like an alien spaceship had landed on Earth. How it looked inside was still unknown.

The fans didn't want to leave after Seattle's Harold Reynolds made the last out in the old park. Nancy Faust played her organ as fans looked out at the field for the last time. People held up signs with messages like "Good-bye Old Friend"; "Thanks for the Memories"; and "Years from Now, We'll Say, We Wuz Here." Tears were everywhere. Fans knew they would never again be able to sit in the same place or the same seat when they saw a dramatic home run, a key strikeout, or a big win. A parking lot would eventually take the place of the beloved old park. (In that parking lot, there is a home plate installed right where the old one sat. Batting boxes are painted into the cement. Anyone who ever attended a game at Old Comiskey can stand there and recall any special memory. Remember. Just remember.)

3. Saying Good-Bye

The players came back onto the field to walk around the outfield and salute the fans. The pain was eased by the fact that the team had its first 90-win season since the 1983 Winning Ugly club. "Doing the Little Things" had become the slogan of the last year at Comiskey. Yes, this White Sox team did the little things. They hit the cutoff man, turned the double play, advanced the runner, drove in the runner from third with less than two outs, and had Bobby Thigpen, who set a record for saves with 57, which held up for 18 years. They did all those things, and they provided great memories of Comiskey's final season. Attendance improved over a million over 1989 and surpassed the two-million mark for the first time since 1984. There couldn't have been a better way to say good-bye.

But even with all the drama, the 1990 season was not over. The White Sox still had three games to play. Although they would lose two of them, the 1990 White Sox demonstrated that they were the best team to play the last game at Comiskey.

The last three games of the season were against the Red Sox in Fenway Park. Boston was in close battle for the AL East with Toronto. They needed to win two of three games against the White Sox to make the playoffs. With two outs in the ninth inning in game three, it appeared the Red Sox would do just that.

The teams had split the first two games. Boston won game one, 4–3, and the White Sox took game two, 3–2, in 11 innings. In the finale, the Red Sox led, 3–1, with two outs in the ninth. Closer Jeff Reardon was on the mound. Red Sox fans were on their feet. Sammy Sosa was at the plate.

At this point, two things need to be said about Sosa. One of the dumbest moves the White Sox ever made was trading him to the Cubs. Could you imagine a lineup with Sosa and Frank Thomas as both matured into great hitters?

Thing number two is that crashing the 60-home run barrier was the worst thing that ever happened to Sosa. Fame is always hard to handle, and he had worldwide adulation. It was all too much. He didn't need to set records to have a great career. He didn't need steroids to have a great career (if indeed he took steroids.) He and Frank Thomas could have led the White Sox to the World Series before

Section One—Overcoming History

2005. He'd be in the Hall of Fame right there with Thomas. Now, that would have been some White Sox history.

Back to Boston and Jeff Reardon. Sosa swung and missed at the first pitch. He fouled off the next offering. One strike to go, and Red Sox fans were cheering. But Sosa picked on an outside breaking pitch and singled to center.

Scott Fletcher was next, and Reardon plunked him on the shoulder. Now the tying run was on first, and the lead run was coming to the plate in the form of Ozzie Guillén. Fenway grew nervous again.

Guillén fouled off pitch number one. He missed the next pitch. One more time, the White Sox were down to the last out and the last strike. Guillén reached for a high pitch and laced it down the right field line. Red Sox fans must have had instant nightmares of the ball rattling around the corner, driving in the tying runs. Right fielder Tom Brunansky saved the day for the Red Sox. He made a diving catch right next to the line, a few feet from the wall. Boston had its division title.

The White Sox lost, but they had fought to the very last strike. They again proved that they had earned the honor of playing the last game in Old Comiskey.

After the game, manager Jeff Torberg talked sadly on WMAQ-670 AM radio. "This was our playoff," he said. It was, and they held up well.

4

◆ ◆ ◆

Ushering in a New Stadium

For the first time since April 20, 1916—when what is now known as Wrigley Field opened as Weeghman Park—there was a new major league stadium in Chicago. On April 18, 1991, the Chicago White Sox played their inaugural game at what was still called Comiskey Park at that time. Over 42,000 fans walked through the turnstiles for a game against the Detroit Tigers on the South Side of Chicago.

Naturally, there was a great deal of anticipation and excitement on many fronts. First, there were the usual high emotions associated with a home opener. In addition, fans were anxious to see what the new ballpark looked like on the inside. I drove by one evening about a month before the opener to see the stadium lights on and illuminating the park. I wondered if the new Comiskey would have the nightly beauty that the first Comiskey had.

How would the overall baseball experience be compared to the park that would soon be torn down? Would this stadium become a symbol of newfound success? Would a World Series finally happen? Would more than one World Series happen? Would any World Series be damaged by scandal? Would it, like the first Comiskey in its day, be considered state of the art, looked upon as an example for the rest of baseball? Or would fans become disillusioned with something their tax dollars helped fund?

The White Sox had just returned from a seven-game road trip and had started the season brightly with a 6–1 mark. In the off-season, the club had added veterans Tim Raines and Charlie Hough. The young Frank Thomas and Robin Ventura looked ready to fully establish themselves as productive major league players. There

Section One—Overcoming History

was also the good feeling left from the over-achieving 1990 season. Everything was so upbeat when ace Jack McDowell threw the first pitch in the new Comiskey Park.

McDowell got through the first two innings without giving up a run, and it looked like it would be another dominating Black Jack performance. Then everything collapsed around him. The Tigers scored six runs in the third inning and a whopping 10 in the fourth. Detroit picked up 15 hits in those first four innings, and the game's suspense evaporated. The White Sox lost their first game in their spanking new stadium, 16–0.

This could not have been in any fantasy of a White Sox player or fan. McDowell told me in an interview 10 years later that he and a few teammates sat around the club house afterward and wondered, "What was that all about?"[1]

McDowell said they had concluded that with the opening of a new stadium, the White Sox had "angered the gods of Old Comiskey." McDowell, Robin Ventura, and relief pitcher Scott Radinsky went out behind second base the next day and burned a uniform in a sacrificial offering to those gods of Old Comiskey. It seemed to work, at least during one play during the second game at the park.

"Rob Deer [Tigers right fielder] stumbled and let a line drive get past him," McDowell said. McDowell was convinced that the gods had been placated by the burning sacrifice even though the Sox lost that game, too. But McDowell maintained that Deer should have and normally would have executed that play. Instead, the gods had intervened. Poor Rob Deer.[2]

Scalping is a tradition associated with many sporting and entertainment events. On some occasions, tickets get bought in bulk and are sold at inflated prices. (In reality, this was an illegal practice, although ticket brokers became commonplace in the 1990s.) During the late 1960s, the average Chicago hockey fan couldn't get a ticket to a Black Hawks game without dealing with a scalper. Scalping didn't happen often with White Sox tickets. Getting a good seat on the day of the game was relatively easy.

That changed somewhat in October 1983 after the White Sox clinched their first division title. A $15 dollar playoff seat was said

4. Ushering in a New Stadium

to be sold on the street for $150. A guy at work tried to hit me up for some big money, and I had no trouble turning him down. I badly wanted to go the playoffs, but not at his gouging prices. It was way out of my league.

For that frustrating game number four against Baltimore, a friend and I decided to go to McCuddy's Bar across the street from Comiskey. We could watch the game on TV, have a few beers, and feel the atmosphere of the ballpark.

As we walked over, a man called out and asked if we had tickets. I yelled back that we couldn't pay whatever he was demanding. He came over and reassured us that he'd be reasonable. A $15 ticket for a seat in right center field would go for $20. We took the deal even though we probably could have gotten them at face value because the first pitch was ten minutes away. But we were so happy to have tickets that we paid the money without negotiation. Thus we got to see a heartbreaking game.

There is an underpass about a block and a half from the ballpark. Many scalping purchases were completed there in 1991. A friend and I went to a night game in August 1991 without tickets. After establishing that I was not a cop, a scalper offered two tickets at three times the face value. I countered with an offer of twice the face value. He wouldn't budge, and my friend and I began walking away. The scalper went into pressure mode. Didn't I want to see the White Sox in the middle of a pennant race? In the new stadium? We kept walking.

We returned to the ballpark. We must have looked like orphans because a man approached and said he had two extra tickets. I asked the price, expecting another gouging. He told me he would give them to us. He said he couldn't use the tickets and didn't care about getting anything for them. He handed me the tickets, and I thanked him profusely.

This provided my first experience with the controversial and very high upper deck. I held onto my seat for the first three innings, as I had the dreadful feeling I was going to fall forward. I imagined myself plummeting over the railing to the lower deck, killing myself and whoever happened to be underneath my suicidal tumble.

In old Comiskey, there were two sets of ramps in the upper deck.

Section One—Overcoming History

If a fan had a seat high up, he/she could use the upper ramp and not have to climb all those steps. The new stadium only had a ramp at the very bottom. If a guy had a prostate problem, I doubted that he could make the long and steep climb down to make it to the rest room. Poor guy with a prostate problem. (Years later, several rows at the top of the upper deck would be eliminated during a structural rehab. It's still a hike to get to the top row, and still a problem for guys with prostate issues like me. Of course, once the prostate guy returned to his seat, it was time to go back down again.)

My last experience with a scalper came during the 1993 ALCS, when the White Sox faced the Toronto Blue Jays. I was meeting a friend and got there first. When I went scouting for tickets, I came across two men who had two upper deck tickets valued at $30. They priced them at $75 each. I countered with $60. They played hardball and stayed at $75. I walked.

I made my way over to the other side of the stadium and ended up on 37th Street. A man stood out in the middle of the street amidst slow-moving traffic heading to the parking lots. This scalper had the same deal. Upper deck seats for $75 each. Again, I offered $60. Once more, my offer was refused. As I started to leave, the man called out, "What if you don't get in?" In a passive tone, I replied, "Then I don't get in." The man relented and sold the tickets for $60 each. I should have negotiated further because he now seemed desperate, but I'm just not good at that sort of thing. But I got my tickets.

I returned to the ballpark in search of my friend. The two original scalpers now approached me with a smile and said they were ready to agree to the $60 price. Their faces fell when I told them I already had tickets. My tone dripped with arrogance. My own face fell when the White Sox lost, 7–3, to Toronto. Just another post-season loss at home, even at the new home, at inflationary prices.

Going to the new Comiskey Park was a different experience in the early 1990s. The team was winning, and tickets were scarce. Dealing with scalpers was almost fun. And, in 1991, for a time, it appeared that the first season at the new Comiskey Park would truly be historic. For a time, it looked like the White Sox would win the AL West, perhaps win a great deal more.

4. Ushering in a New Stadium

The American League West was an oddly deep division in 1991. At the end of the season, no team would have a losing record. The last-place team, California, finished a dead even 81–81. Oakland was still a good club, but far from the dominant team it had been in the late 1980s. The White Sox seemed to be in a good position to take the division title even though the Twins were having a great year.

On the last night of July, Robin Ventura hit a walk-off grand slam off Goose Gossage to beat the Rangers, 10–8. The next day, the Sox romped to another win over Texas, 13–2, and stood only two games behind first-place Minnesota. That win completed an eight-game winning streak.

On August 11, the White Sox played the third of a four-game series in Baltimore. They were on another hot streak, having won six straight. Twenty-one-year-old lefty Wilson Álvarez was making his first start for the Sox.

Álvarez was part of one of the best trades a White Sox front office ever made. The Sox sent Harold Baines and infielder Fred Manrique to Texas for Álvarez, Sammy Sosa, and Scott Fletcher. To say the least, Texas came up short on this one. The Rangers didn't even bother to hold onto Baines.

Álvarez had only one other appearance before this Baltimore game and didn't even get one out. On July 24, 1989, against Toronto, he gave up three hits and two walks in the first inning and took an early exit. But he was only 18 at the time and no doubt was up in the big leagues too soon.

His first inning against the Orioles was far different. A pumped-up Álvarez struck out the side. Cal Ripken, Jr., was his third victim.

The Sox scored two runs in the first inning on an opposite-field home run by Frank Thomas. Thomas almost got another homer in the second and ended up with a double. The Sox added two more runs. By the bottom of the seventh inning, they led, 7–0. Along with this comfortable lead, rookie Wilson Álvarez was throwing a no-hitter.

In the Baltimore seventh with one out, Ripken dribbled a grounder that barely inched its way down the third base line. Álvarez

Section One—Overcoming History

went to field the ball, but catcher Ron Karkovice called him off the play. Karkovice's throw to first was high and wild, and Ripken ended up on second base. Was this play a hit or an error?

On the WGN-TV replay, it clearly showed that an accurate throw would have gotten Ripken. Yet this had not been an easy play. The official scorer's decision was made quickly: error. The Baltimore crowd cheered, as it would cheer Álvarez for the remainder of the game.

This call could have gone either way. Perhaps the scorer felt for Álvarez, and how could he take a pitcher's no-hitter away on a topped ball that didn't go more than 20 feet? Regardless, Álvarez got out of the inning with his no-hitter still intact.

Chris Hoiles led off the Orioles' eighth, and it appeared that he had broken through with a hit. Hoiles lifted a soft fly that looked like it would drop in in right-center. Center fielder Lance Johnson hustled in, caught the ball inches above the grass, and somersaulted. When he hit the ground, he looked like a human pretzel. Johnson held up his glove to show the umpire he had made the catch. To say the least, it was a great defensive play. The no-hitter was still there.

Things looked bright for Álvarez in the ninth as he got the first two hitters out. But he appeared to start overthrowing his pitches as he attempted to get that last out to secure the no-hitter. He walked Ripken and Dwight Evans. He wasn't all that close as his offerings sailed way outside.

Ozzie Guillén came in from shortstop to talk to Álvarez. Both men are from Venezuela, so Guillén was the perfect person to conduct this mound conference. Same countrymen, same language. Also, Guillén was the veteran reaching out to the rookie. This was one of the great moments in Guillén's career.

I don't know what Guillén said, but Álvarez found the plate again. He struck out Randy Milligan on a nasty breaking pitch that dropped about two feet. The Orioles fans cheered the no-hitter.

Álvarez didn't know how to react. At first, he showed no glee or any emotion. It had to be overwhelming. Second major league start. New team. New country. His teammates knew how to react: they ran out to mob him in celebration. At only 21 years old, Wilson Álvarez had already achieved a great milestone. A little over two years later,

4. Ushering in a New Stadium

Álvarez didn't look quite so overwhelmed when he beat Toronto in the fourth game of the 1993 ALCS.

Everything was going great for the White Sox. They won their seventh straight game and 15th out of their last 17. Only one game separated them from the first-place Twins. Could they do it? Could they win a championship in the first year in the new ballpark?

Chicago Sun-Times columnist Richard Roeper was brimming with optimism in his next day's column. He predicted that Frank Thomas would hit 500 home runs for the White Sox and that the 1991 club was a "team of destiny." (In his Hall of Fame career, Frank Thomas hit 521 home runs, tying Ted Williams and Willie McCovey. He hit 448 of those 521 home runs for the White Sox. Would the White Sox become a team of destiny in 1991? Not so much.)

After winning 15 of 17, the White Sox lost 15 of 17. A little more than two weeks after the Álvarez no-hitter, the Sox were no-hit themselves. Bret Saberhagen of the Royals did the trick as Kansas City won by the identical score of the Álvarez game, 7–0. Saberhagen walked two in the contest.

There was one tough call for the scorer in the fifth inning. Dan Pasqua hit a routine-looking fly to left. Kirk Gibson misjudged it somewhat and had it tip off the edge of his glove for a two-base error. It had barely nicked Gibson's glove, but maybe the scorer called it an error because Gibson looked so bad. Or maybe he was being generous to Saberhagen. At any rate, the Sox never got close to getting a hit after that. Even TV play-by-play man Hawk Harrelson thought the Sox had no chance to break through with a hit.

In the end, there were more important things. The White Sox were in the middle of a nine-game losing streak. By the time the streak ended, the Sox were nine games behind the Twins and had dropped to third place. They were on the wrong end of destiny. Their championship dreams had been vaporized.

Yet on September 2, Roberto Hernández started in the first game of his career when he pitched for the White Sox against Kansas City in the new ballpark. Just months before, Hernández had to have two surgeries on his pitching arm to repair blood clots. The two surgeries took a combined 15 hours.

Section One—Overcoming History

For a time, it looked like Hernández would duplicate the Álvarez feat. He took a no-hitter into the seventh inning. But Royals infielder Bill Pecota doubled to start the seventh. The White Sox won the game, 5–1, giving Hernández the first win of his career. Eventually, Hernández became the Sox closer and the centerpiece of a controversial trade. In his career, all but three games as a reliever, he'd appear in 1,010 games and pick up 326 saves.

After the Hernández win, the White Sox climbed back into second place, but it was a small consolation. They were 8½ games behind the Twins, and a division title was not at all likely.

Despite the late-season swoon, the White Sox still ended up with the third-best record in the American League. The Twins went to and won a dramatic World Series against Atlanta. Could that have been the White Sox celebrating instead of the Twins? Celebrating in their new stadium, creating a new tradition? Wouldn't that have been a great way to christen their new ballpark?

As in the passing decades, White Sox fans searched for answers. Just what happened after the Álvarez no-hitter? Just what happened to all that momentum? What about Richard Roeper? Wasn't he right about everything?

The White Sox did set a Chicago baseball attendance record that year with 2,934,154 fans paying their way into the new Comiskey Park. (Scalpers prospered.) Additionally, the team still had talent. Maybe next year? No, not next year either.

5

♦ ♦ ♦

Bo Knows Baseball

The scene was in a banquet room at the Palmer House Hotel in downtown Chicago on January 23, 1993. It was a typically ice-cold January night with the wind whipping off Lake Michigan. At that time, Chicago area sportswriters hosted what they called the "Diamond Dinner" every January. They would honor White Sox and Cubs players, past and present, along with a player they labeled as a "World Series hero." A little over 1,000 fans would show up, talk about baseball, get an autograph or two, and look forward to the upcoming baseball season while enjoying a nice dinner.

Bo Jackson was at the microphone. He was being honored for his comeback efforts after suffering a hip injury playing for the Oakland Raiders in a playoff game on January 13, 1991. Jackson was the extremely rare athlete who played in two major league sports. His NFL career was over, as was his time with the Kansas City Royals, but he was still attempting to make a comeback in major league baseball. In 1991, he had 71 at-bats for the White Sox but sat out the 1992 season as he continued to rehab after hip surgery. He now looked forward to playing for the Sox in 1993.

Looking out over the audience that night, Jackson said he wanted to introduce his "date." He asked White Sox trainer Herm Schneider to stand up and be recognized. The shy Schneider didn't react. Jackson stared at the audience again, this time searching for Schneider. His hardened expression showed his displeasure. Then, in a booming and deep voice, Jackson yelled out, "I SAID STAND UP." Apparently, Schneider finally complied although I didn't spot him in the dense audience. But Jackson had been so intimidating, I had almost stood up.

Section One—Overcoming History

Jackson's hip injury had resulted in a medical condition known as avascular necrosis.[1] Avascular necrosis is medically described as the death of bone tissue due to temporary or permanent loss of blood supply to the bone. According to Dr. Praldeep Sharma, the following activities should be stopped or at least limited: smoking, excessive walking, physiotherapy, yoga asanas, gymming, sitting cross legged, squatting, energy powers, and biking. (treatavn.com/blog)

Nothing was said about not playing major league baseball.

The Kansas City Royals had released Jackson before the 1991 season, thinking he would never play baseball again. The White Sox signed him on April 3, although they didn't think he would play that season.

"Right now, I feel like a caged animal," Jackson said at a press conference. "I can't wait for them to open chutes and let me go and do what I've been doing my whole life and that's running."[2]

In the film produced by Nike titled "Bo Knows Bo—Pro Baseball," other major league players are shown expressing skepticism about Jackson early in his baseball career. What was a football player doing trying to play baseball? Their viewpoints change as images of Jackson's major league baseball accomplishments are shown. Skepticism turns to amazement.

Jackson's first major league home run came on September 14, 1986. Playing for the Royals, Jackson hit a drive to straightaway center off of Seattle's Mike Moore. It landed way up on the grass of the hitting backdrop. The homer was estimated at a prodigious 475 feet, and the Nike film stated that it was the longest in Kauffman Stadium history, at least at that point.

On July 11, 1989, in the All-Star Game in Anaheim, Jackson hit another home run that was also estimated at 475 feet. It came off Giants pitcher Rick Reuschel. In the second inning, Jackson easily beat out an attempted double play after he grounded to short. This allowed a run to score from third, giving Jackson another RBI. He singled to center in his next at-bat. Eventually he ended up on second base and advanced to third on a medium fly to center. Jackson was so quick that the outfielder didn't bother to challenge him with a throw. He went into third with a head-first slide when he could have gone in standing up. He was named the All-Star Game MVP.

5. Bo Knows Baseball

The Nike clip also shows great defensive outfield plays made by Jackson. It begins with running, leaping grabs. Other plays show a drive heading toward the gap, and Jackson coming out of nowhere to make a lunging catch. Finally, the focus shifts to a Jackson inside-the-park home run when the play at the plate isn't close.

The narration again changes to the once-skeptical players describing Jackson with jaw-dropping amazement. In addition, they voiced their professional respect for Jackson as they praised his work ethic and superior efforts on the field.

Jackson's football injury occurred when he took a pitchout, burst through a large hole at the scrimmage line, turned the corner, and raced up field. He was tackled from behind on what looked like a normal football play. But he seemed to land wrong, and of course, the human body is not meant to take the punishment of a football game.

Jackson did play some baseball for the White Sox in late 1991 but logged only 71 at-bats. Hip surgery followed, and he used the 1992 season to rehab. His NFL career was over, but he still hoped to return to baseball.

Jackson was a feel-good story. The White Sox were giving him a chance just to return to playing baseball. (Royals fans had not been happy with Jackson playing in the NFL and jeopardizing his baseball career. It was worsened by the fact that Jackson was playing for the Kansas City Chiefs' archrival, Oakland.)

Jackson made his first plate appearance in 1993 in the White Sox home opener on April 9 against the Yankees. New York led, 7–4, with one out in the bottom of the sixth inning. Jackson pinch-hit for left-handed-hitting Dan Pasqua, facing southpaw Neal Heaton. Going with an outside breaking pitch, Jackson sent a deep and high drive to right field. It disappeared well into the seats for a home run in his first at-bat of the year, and first since late September 1991.

The center field scoreboard shot off its fireworks as Jackson rounded the bases. He got a big hug from Ozzie Guillén on entering the dugout. He tipped his hat to cheering fans to complete the dramatic moment. "When it left the bat, I thought I popped it up," Jackson would recall. "And the higher it got, I thought it might have a chance, As I rounded second, I got teary-eyed. The only thing I could

Section One—Overcoming History

think about was my mom. I promised her before she left that I would return to baseball. That first hit would be for her."[3]

Jackson said he was also grateful for the reception he got from Guillén. Guillén had missed almost the entire 1982 season because of a knee injury. Jackson said Guillén knew what it was like to go through a long rehab to return to playing.

The White Sox lost that opener, but it didn't matter much to the fans. Bo Jackson had homered on what had to be considered a triumphant return. Jackson would hit an even more dramatic home run later in the season. It would be another memorable and emotional moment of his one full season with the White Sox as fans hoped for a long-awaited World Series appearance. If the hope was realized, it would be the first such appearance in 34 years.

The 1993 team was assembled due to a rebuilding program the franchise went through during the late 1980s. The Winning Ugly Team had lost players to injury, retirement, and decline of baseball skills. The team slowly began to accumulate young players through trades and smart draft choices. They even had Sammy Sosa for a time before trading him to the Cubs.

Draft pick Frank Thomas came up to the White Sox in late summer 1990. Right from the start, the first baseman showed what kind of special hitter he would be. In a game against Toronto on August 13, Thomas faced Blue Jays reliever Duane Ward with two outs and a man on second in the eighth inning. Ward threw a high fast ball in on Thomas to keep him from extending his arms to drive the ball. Not only did Thomas use his strength to extend his arms with an inside-out swing, he hit a rope of a line drive to right center to pick up a clutch RBI. One could say this was a rare demonstration of hitting ability, but Thomas did things like this many times in his career. In his first 191 major league at-bats, Thomas hit .330 and drove in 31 runs. Thomas would always hit for average and power and to all fields.

Draft pick Robin Ventura's first game was on September 12, 1989. Ventura hit .178 in his 45 at-bats that season. However, in 1991, he picked up his first 100-plus RBI season and earned his first Gold Glove for his play at third base. He would earn six Gold Gloves in his 16-year career.

5. Bo Knows Baseball

Draft pick Jack McDowell was in his second full season with the Sox in 1990. He won the last game at old Comiskey for his 14th win of that season. He gave up 10 hits in eight innings but limited the Seattle Mariners to one run.

"It never bothered me that I had a high ratio of hits to innings," he told me some years later. "I didn't worry about spinning a two-hitter. Just keep throwing strikes and you don't get hurt."[4] He walked only one in that last, tear-jerker Comiskey game.

In first place with a three-game lead, the White Sox travelled to Minneapolis for a three-game weekend series starting on August 20, 1993. The *Minneapolis Star Tribune* ran a feature story on the front page of its sports section on Frank Thomas. In a glowing piece, the writer said it was scary and speculated that he would only get better. He already had 32 homers when his team arrived in the Twin Cities.

The Sox took the first two games. In the first inning of the concluding game, Thomas hit his 33rd homer.

The Twins played in the Metrodome back then. Baseball sounds were easier to pick up in the indoor stadium. Thomas' hit made an echoing sound as it took off for left-center field. The home run would be the only run the Sox scored on that rainy afternoon.

Jack McDowell was on the mound. The Twins hit line shots that also echoed as they were sprayed all over the outfield. In the second inning, Minnesota had runners on first and second with one out. In the fourth inning, they had a runner on third with one out. In the sixth, they had runners on first and third with no outs. In the seventh, the situation repeated itself as the Twins again put runners on first and third with none out.

But not one Twin crossed the plate.

In the seventh inning, David McCarty hit into a double play to end the inning. Sox shortstop Craig Grebeck stepped on second for the first out, but his hurried throw to first pulled Thomas off the bag. Thomas was never known for his defense, but he made an athletic-looking tag of McCarty. Another threat had ended with the frustrated Twins missing out on yet another scoring opportunity.

Years later, McDowell told me, "Roberto Hernández [Sox closer in 1993] used to say, 'Black Jack is pitching today. The bullpen can

Section One—Overcoming History

take a day off.' A leader gives that type of effort. You raise the bar a little and that what separates the great and the .500 pitcher."[5]

That day the bullpen got another rest. McDowell pitched a complete game, getting the side in order in both the eighth and ninth innings. Black Jack, as he was nicknamed, struck out Shane Mack with a nasty breaking pitch to end the contest. The strikeout was his tenth.

The victory was McDowell's 20th, and it marked the second consecutive season he reached the 20-win mark. He was the only Sox pitcher to win 20 since LaMarr Hoyt and Richard Dotson accomplished that feat in the Winning Ugly year of 1983. At this point, the White Sox had a four-game lead over second-place Kansas City.

Going into the September 19 game against the A's in Oakland, Texas had replaced the Royals as the closest pursuer. The A's had won the division with 96 wins the year before but now had fallen all the way down to last place. This was a tightly played game, however, with the score tied, 1–1, in the top of the ninth.

Future Hall of Famer Dennis Eckersley was pitching for the A's. With this game, Eckersley became the 19th pitcher in major league history to make an 800th pitching appearance. Since 1988, he had been the dominant reliever in the American League after being a starter earlier in his career, which included almost three seasons with the Cubs.

Frank Thomas started the inning with a single. Robin Ventura followed with a drive to right-center on a pitch that Eckersley left out over the plate. Ventura's drive cleared the wall by plenty just to the right of the 400-foot sign. The Sox had a 3–1 lead.

Reliever Roberto Hernández was able to close out the ninth inning, and the White Sox had an important win. Texas lost that day as the Rangers blew a late-inning lead in Anaheim. But the Rangers were still within striking distance. Beating Eckersley was huge.

On September 27, the 26th anniversary of "Black Wednesday," the Sox magic number stood at one. Seattle had come to Chicago to play at the three-year-old stadium that was still called Comiskey Park. In a pitcher's duel between Wilson Álvarez and Dave Fleming, there was still no score in the bottom of the sixth inning.

5. Bo Knows Baseball

There were two outs and two on. Bo Jackson stepped up and sent a deep fly to left. Outfielder Brian Turang drifted back to the warning track, moved to his right, and edged back to the wall. At first, it appeared he was preparing to make the catch, but he had run out of room. The high drive landed well into the seats for a three-run homer, giving the Sox a 3–0 lead.

Jackson got another emotional greeting from Ozzie Guillén on entering the dugout. The capacity crowd waved white towels and cheered until Jackson stepped out of the dugout for a curtain call. He saluted the crowd with an intense hand signal.

Later, Jackson said, as he did with his first homer of the season, that he thought he had popped the ball up. He probably did some, but he was so strong he was still able to knock it out of the ballpark. It was another big moment for the man who had overcome such odds just to play baseball again.[6]

The White Sox held on to win, 4–2, and clinched the division when Seattle catcher Dave Valle made the last out by hitting a routine fly to Ellis Burks in right. It was the first division title for the club in 10 years.

An elated Jackson did a victory lap around the ballpark, acknowledging happy and cheering fans as he made his way along the warning track. Of course, the division title meant a great deal to every Sox player, but hitting the game-winning homer was special for a player who had wanted to thank his "date" back in the wintertime.

It would have been great for Jackson and the White Sox if they had advanced past the Blue Jays in the ALCS to get into the World Series. But in Game 5, with the series tied at two games apiece, the Blue Jays led, 5–1, in the ninth inning in Toronto. Tim Raines led off for the Sox with a single to right, his 11th hit of the series. But Joey Cora and Frank Thomas both struck out. The loud Toronto crowd got on its feet in anticipation of reliever Duane Ward closing out the game.

Robin Ventura stepped up and quieted the crowd down with a two-run homer into the second deck in right field. Ellis Burks was next, and he got hit by a pitch on a full count. Suddenly, Ward seemed to have lost his command. Now the crowd was not only quiet but nervous.

Section One—Overcoming History

Who was coming up next, representing the tying run? Bo Jackson. Could he have another story book moment with another big hit?

With a viscous swing, Jackson fouled off a hanging breaking pitch on a one-and-one count. It was easy to see his frustration as he stepped out of the box. He had a pitch to hit, and he missed it.

Could Bo still do it? Not on the next pitch. He swung and missed for strike three. Toronto eliminated the Sox in the next game in Chicago. The White Sox had lost three of their home games in the series, extending their home post-season losing streak to seven.

Bo Jackson proved to be human, but that made his story all the more appealing. His path back to the majors was still inspiring as he was very human, not just a superstar who did amazing things. He'd play one more year with the Angels before leaving baseball.

As for the White Sox, they were still a young and talented team with or without Bo Jackson. But now they had had a taste of post-season play. Their fans could truly say, "wait till next year" when it came to 1994. Couldn't they? Couldn't they?

6

♦ ♦ ♦

A New Way of Not Going to the World Series

Baseball strikes and the White Sox are funny things. The Sox had optimistically looked forward to the opening of the 1972 season. In the off-season, they had acquitted Dick Allen, a Bo Jackson–type player who could hit with devastating power. (Every home run Allen hit at old Comiskey Park was awe-inspiring and truly memorable. A fan really hasn't seen a home run unless he or she has seen a Dick Allen home run.) He could also steal a base, hit over .300, and play a good first base. He won National League Rookie of the Year honors in 1964 when he piled up 201 hits along with 29 homers and 91 RBI.

Allen was not the type of player the Sox traditionally had on their roster. Even during their most successful years, the team's success was tied to solid pitching, defense, and the ability to manufacture runs. Superstars and marquee players were on other teams. But on December 2, 1971, general manager Roland Hemond decided to trade a solid starting pitcher, Tommy John, to get Allen, even though Allen had been considered a malcontent on other teams. Talent was talent.

Although 1971 had not been a great season, the Sox had rebounded somewhat from a 106-loss year in 1970 to end up just four wins under .500. Left-handed knuckleballer Wilbur Wood won 22 games, and third baseman Bill Melton won the American League home run championship on the last day of the season. (Melton was the first White Sox player to win a home run championship and the first to hit 30 home runs in a season, totaling 33.) Now it was time for the improving team to take a large step forward and contend for the American League West Division title. Maybe even a World Series? A player like Dick Allen could lead the way.

According to Hemond, the team expected a crowd nearing 50,000 to attend the home opener on April 6. Attendance had sagged dramatically in the recent losing years, and now it appeared that the franchise could rebuild its fan base. With Allen and Melton batting three-four in the lineup, it looked like the opener could be an historic day for a team that had had four consecutive losing seasons in front of a sea of empty seats.

But there was no home opener on April 6. In fact, no one played major league baseball anywhere. There was a work stoppage over the issue of increasing contributions to the players' union's pension fund. Comiskey Park remained empty.

Fortunately, the work stoppage, which technically was a player lockout, lasted only 13 days. Unfortunately for the White Sox, however, their home opener was played on a cold and damp Tuesday night on April 18. Only 20,493 spectators attended. But the game was still a success. The White Sox won, 14–0, with Allen picking up two hits and two RBI. Even when Allen made an out in the seventh inning, he used his powerful, down-cutting swing to fly out to the deepest part of the park in right-center. Wilbur Wood showed his 1971 form by throwing a complete game three-hitter.

Most importantly, 1972 was a great year for the team even though they lost Bill Melton to a back injury. Allen had an MVP year, hitting 37 homers and driving in 113 runs. The White Sox finished in second place, only 5½ games behind Oakland. They had their best attendance in six years, topping the million mark for the first time since 1966. The work stoppage, though not timely, had no long-lasting effect on the White Sox, although it would have given the franchise a shot in the arm to have a capacity crowd on Opening Day.

In 1981, optimism reigned again. The team had a miserable decade during the 1970s, achieving only two winning seasons. But a new group headed by Jerry Reinsdorf and Eddie Einhorn had purchased the team from the financially strapped Bill Veeck in January.

6. A New Way of Not Going to the World Series

Recognizing they had to establish credibility with a cynical fan base, the new ownership acquired Carlton Fisk and Greg Luzinski, adding them to a group of developing young players. A winning home opener on April 14 was attended by 51,560. Fans began believing again.

On June 11, the Sox beat the Yankees, 3–2, in front of another good crowd of 33,777. Their record stood at 31–22, only 2½ games out of first place. The team appeared to have come out of the darkness of the losing 1970s and into the light of the hopefully winning 1980s.

They would not play another game for two months.

There was another work stoppage, this time over compensation for free agents. In my opinion, as a former labor reporter, this stupid action could have been averted with common sense negotiating.. Instead baseball was taken away from the fans during the peak summer season. The White Sox barely played .500 ball during the second half, and the season had a disappointing ending. It would have been nice to see the team develop over a regular, 162-game season. Fans were returning, only to see Comiskey Park go dark during a good deal of the summertime.

On August 10, 1994, the White Sox beat the A's, 2–1, in Oakland. The young right-hander, Jason Bere, improved his record to 12–2. It was the last game the White Sox played that season. Another work stoppage began, only this time it would do more than push back a home opener or cancel games in the middle of the summer. The strike would have a devastating effect on a franchise that was still trying to find a winning identity.

This was the strike that would end the season without a post-season. As play ended for good, the Sox led the newly formed American League Central Division. The division race looked to be exciting. Cleveland sat in second place, one game out, and a hot Kansas City team was four games behind. The wild card system was in its first year, and even if the Sox didn't win their division, it appeared they still would get into the playoffs somehow. The newly built Comiskey Park, only in its fourth season, was packed every game. Scalpers were still making money. The White Sox had to be making money. The team was winning. Things were good.

Section One—Overcoming History

Now, if you ask any fan what the major sticking points in the negotiations were in 1994, he/she probably couldn't tell you. Two stumbling blocks involved arbitration and a salary cap. What most fans remember is the frustrating feeling stemming from two sides making money not finding common ground. The fan will recall that there was no World Series for the first time in 90 years. They will also recall voicing their anger and dissent, but they were ignored, and the season ended with a disappointing thud.

What is remembered as well, with true bitterness, is that there were opportunities for dramatic baseball history to be made. Matt Williams of the Giants had 43 home runs, and fans looked forward to seeing him have a shot at 60. Tony Gwynn of the Padres was hitting .394, and fans wanted to see him have a shot at .400. Frank Thomas was contending for the American League Triple Crown. A potentially record-breaking and historic season became meaningless.

The Montreal Expos were hit the hardest by the strike. The Expos had the best record in the major leagues. For the first time since the team's inception in 1969, it appeared that the Expos would go to the World Series. Many observers thought they would win it. But, of course, there was no World Series, not in Montreal, not anywhere.

Upon returning after the strike, the Expos franchise sold off a good deal of its talent. In 1995, they looked like the normal losing Expos, finishing last. By 2005, the team moved to Washington, D.C., and became the Nationals. The Nationals finally won the World Series in 2019, the 50th anniversary of the Expos' entrance into the National League. Canada still has only one major league baseball team, and that team hasn't gone to a World Series since 1993.

In most accounts describing the effects of the 1994–1995 strike, the emphasis is on Williams, Gwynn, and the Expos. Some had even crowed about the Yankees returning to the post-season. The White Sox, however, seem to be forgotten by history even though the strike had a more devastating impact on the franchise, damage that in some ways still endures, even at this writing.

Everything had been progressing so well. Frank Thomas already had 38 homers. Off-season pickup Julio Franco already had 98 RBI.

6. A New Way of Not Going to the World Series

Their late-1980s' rebuilding program was working as young players became more experienced. The championship window was open, and all the Sox had to do was make their way through. Instead, the window was slowly closing as the season slipped away into a dubious history. The Sox still had had only one World Series appearance since 1919. The Reinsdorf-Einhorn ownership had controlled the team for 14 seasons, and the promise of a championship still had not been fulfilled. The honeymoon was over. "I don't want to go out," Reinsdorf said two weeks before play stopped. "I really don't. There is no gain for us. Even if we get everything we were looking for, whatever we save in the cap, we lose in revenue sharing. The best deal is for us to keep playing."[1]

Reinsdorf sounded conciliatory and even described himself as a "dove." But later he accused the union of not taking the owners' demands seriously, said that most teams were losing money, and, if the players walked out, he would become a "hawk." The "hawk" reference would come back to haunt him as fans began to think he was a driving force behind the owners' decision to cancel the post-season. Some came to think he didn't care about winning and that making money was his only concern. How about making money *and* winning?[2]

On September 14, after a 26–2 vote, the owners announced that the 1994 season was over. All remaining games had been wiped off the schedule, because according to Commissioner Bud Selig, the players union had not responded "in any meaningful way" to owners' demands and concerns about containing operating costs. Players union head Donald Fehr had a different take. "When people think back to what the final image of the 1994 season will be," Fehr said, "it may be Bud Selig at a press conference in Milwaukee protesting pain and gnashing teeth but nevertheless going ahead and dashing the hopes of many people. It was their decision to make. They decided their circumstances were more important."[3]

In early October 1973, I drove past old Comiskey in the early part of a fall evening. The setting sun peeked through the upper deck in a prism-like way, but the aging park looked desolate and lonely. One more time the playoffs had begun without the White Sox, and it didn't look like they would go to the post-season any time soon.

55

Section One—Overcoming History

Nearly 21 years later, in an AP photograph taken by Timothy Boyce, Frank Thomas was shown taking his belongings out of the new Comiskey Park as the 1994 strike had started. He tried to look cheerful, smiling in the early evening. But once again, the sun was setting on the Sox, and their new stadium looked desolate and lonely under a darkening sky.

This was a new way for the Chicago White Sox not to go to the World Series ... the most frustrating way. The sun would set on the franchise for a while.

In January 1995, the White Sox organization ran an advertisement in both Chicago daily newspapers asking fans to write in with their views on the strike. Or they could write about anything. The ad was written and formatted in this way:

> WE'VE HEARD FROM THE PLAYERS
> WE'VE HEARD FROM THE OWNERS
> WE'VE HEARD FROM TED KOPPEL
> IT'S TIME WE'VE HEARD FROM YOU
> WRITE US WHAT YOU REALLY THINK
> WRITE US IF YOU MISS BASEBALL
> WRITE US IF YOU DON'T
> WRITE US ABOUT GOING TO GAMES AS A KID
> WRITE US AND TELL US TO GO TO BLAZES
> WRITE US HOW UNCLE BERNIE LIKES HIS NEW TRAILER HOME
> WRITE US SOMETHING

I responded with a letter, although I wondered if anyone in the White Sox organization really cared what one fan like me thought. Or even what a number of fans like me thought. In my letter, I stated that Chicago wasn't built only by industrialists—it was also built by craftsmen and laborers. I also stated that while the players' union was different from other unions, it was still a union, and it had a right to represent its members' interests.

In addition, I explained that I had been a member of the United Steelworkers Union during the 1980s. In a contract signed in 1983, the union gave the steel industry $6 billion in concessions. What did union members get in return? Industry contraction and more job loss. Why should any union agree to any kind of concession package when it would only be betraying its members? I ended the

6. A New Way of Not Going to the World Series

correspondence by suggesting that the owners do some serious negotiating so the 1995 season could start on time.

I received a reply from White Sox PR man Rob Gallas. To give him credit, it was no form letter. From appearances, he had taken time to read my letter. He acknowledged my points and even stated that he was impressed with my views on unions.

To my knowledge, the White Sox never publicly stated the overall consensus of the letters they had received. Eventually they put out a small publication entitled, "Dear Sox," in which fans wrote about happy memories of attending games. I do not know how many letters directly answered the advertisement or how many appeared in "Dear Sox."

Did these letters have any effect? That is also unknown. But in the spring of 1995, the owners played some hardball.

In an abstract titled "Permanent Replacements and the End of Labors [sic] Only True Weapon," John Logan wrote, "the use and threatened use of permanent replacement workers during economic strikes has been one of the most devastating antiunion tactics used by American employers in recent years."[4]

That "devastating antiunion tactic" is just what the MLB owners turned to during spring training in 1995. The teams brought in "replacement players."

In an August 12, 2019, story in the *Los Angeles Times* that looked back at the strike, Mike DiGiovanna wrote, "The left-hander who works in the car-detailing business zipped a fast ball into the mitt of the Home Depot department manager, and with that, the Angels 1995 spring training camp was in full swing."[5]

Although DiGiovanna's story started out in a whimsical way, he also included a serious reflection from Bill Bavasi, who was the Angels' general manager in 1995. "Replacement-player baseball," Bavasi said, "was definitely a blight on a lot of our careers."[6] Baltimore owner Peter Angelos would not field a replacement team, saying that anyone thinking fans would accept the replacements was "obviously suffering hallucinations."[7]

A few years later, the *Seinfeld* sitcom made fun of sports fans, saying they "cheered for laundry." *Seinfeld* had a point. However,

Section One—Overcoming History

White Sox fans would have eventually noticed that Frank Thomas was not at first base, Robin Ventura was not at third, and no one resembling Jack McDowell was on the pitcher's mound.

But using replacement players no doubt had strong appeal to the owners. Unions in general had been on the political defensive since President Reagan had fired all the air traffic controllers in September 1981. In 1987, replacement players helped owners break the NFL players' strike, with that union winning none of its demands. This occurred despite the fact that replacement games were poorly attended. And those replacement results were counted in the standings.

But the Major League Baseball Players Association had remained strong during years of labor setbacks and the falling percentage of unionized workers in the country's workforce. It is highly unlikely that using replacement players would have broken the 1994–1995 strike. By using this dubious strategy, the owners demonstrated that they had underestimated the strength and discipline of the players' union.

In late March 1995, the National Labor Relations Board ruled that the MLB owners had not negotiated in good faith. Federal judge Sonia Sotomayor, now a Supreme Court judge, issued an injunction restoring the expired collective bargaining agreement. The strike was over, and the White Sox would play their first game on April 26.

Because of the late start, the schedule was reduced to 144 games. The work stoppage settled nothing, making the whole process a joke. A post-season had been lost, and the owners and players *still* had to resolve their differences and ratify a new contract.

In an article published on YahooSports.com, Hannah Keyser looked back at the strike on its 15th anniversary in 2009. She quoted a cynical *Dayton Daily News* writer named D.L. Stewart as he observed the strike's dynamics in 1994.

> If the fans *really* think the stupid greedy owners are making too much money, there is a simple answer. Stop buying tickets. If the fans *really* think that the stupid greedy players are making too much money, there is a simple answer. Stop buying tickets.
>
> It's never going to happen. Fans talk about how they're never going to

6. A New Way of Not Going to the World Series

another game because it's nothing but big business and not the innocent pastime it used to be when they were kids.

But they're going.[8]

If the major league baseball industry agreed with Stewart and thought fans would return and everything would go back to normal, they and Stewart were seriously mistaken. They realized baseball was a business and not a pastime. Some fans obviously returned, but overall attendance was not good, and the fans who went to games vented their anger. Some of that anger led to the Ozzie Guillén "we don't owe the fans anything," remark, a remark that only fueled that anger no matter why Guillén said it.

In White Sox history dating back to the beginning of the 20th century, the club had never won back-to back pennants or division titles. (They still haven't.) Team television advertisements in early 1995 pointed out that the Sox had won back-to-back division titles in 1993 and 1994. Technically true, but fans were not impressed. Divisions are not won in August. Bragging about this accomplishment only reminded fans that the 1994 season had been left unfinished, and any title from that year was meaningless. The franchise no longer lists 1994 as a division-winning season. It now knows better.

The White Sox might have handled the fan anger better if they had had a better season in 1995. Instead, they got off to a horrendous start and never played .500 ball. They finished in third place, a whopping 32 games behind division-winning Cleveland. What had happened to that championship window?

I had no intention of attending a game in 1995. Apparently, the White Sox realized many fans like me were going to do the same thing no matter what D.L. Stewart wrote. Since I had answered their newspaper advertisement asking for feedback, the organization sent me four tickets. That way I could go to a game without spending money on the White Sox.

I took my brother and his two sons to the July 12 game against the Brewers. The Sox played well and won, 8–2, behind the pitching of Wilson Álvarez. A little over 21,000 fans attended, but the quiet crowd was spread out over the large stadium, making it look empty. From 1991 through 1994, average Sox attendance ranged

Section One—Overcoming History

from 30,000 to 36,000 a game. In 1995, it shrank to little over 22,000. The consequences of the strike were ongoing. D.L. Stewart had been wrong. Many fans were not returning to buy tickets.

Would the White Sox have won the 1994 World Series? They had a slim lead in their division, and the Yankees looked strong that year. Many observers thought the Expos had to be the favorite to win everything. While attending a 25th anniversary reunion of the 1993 division champs, Jack McDowell claimed the 1994 team had had what it took to win the elusive championship. "Alex [Fernandez] struggled in the first half of the season," he said. "Who were our all-star pitchers? Jason and Wilson [Bere and Álvarez]. They kept up their good year. By the end of the year, Alex and I were really dealing."[9]

Jack McDowell was a tough competitor, so it makes sense he would say something like this. Yet the Sox had gone 24–14 in the last weeks before the strike. They had a chance to do something that hadn't happened for the club in 77 years. But they never got that chance, and that was what bothered fans the most. Not knowing what would have happened was maddening. And that nagging and maddening feeling fueled an anger that was only mounting.

7

♦ ♦ ♦

Backlash

Trades in the major leagues are often controversial. Fans can get emotional when a favorite player is dealt away, or they may anguish over what they think is a bad deal for their team. Some lopsided trades (like Lou Brock for Ernie Broglio in 1964, for example) are remembered for decades. But for the most part, fans will forget about (or at least chill out about) trades as time passes as they become more distracted by the present.

On this subject, one trade stands out as something truly unique, and it is associated with the White Sox. It became known and remains known as the "White Flag Trade."

On July 31, 1997, the White Sox sent three veteran players, all pitchers, to the San Francisco Giants for six unknowns. Now, trading veterans for prospects is nothing new. The White Sox made a somewhat convincing argument that they would not have been able to sign these veterans after the 1997 season, so it only made sense to get something for them instead of seeing their roster gutted.

Additionally, it makes sense for a non-contending team to get a head start on a rebuilding program. The only problem was that the White Sox *were* in contention. Their record was a very average one win under .500, but they were only 3½ games behind first-place Cleveland. Along with that, they had been playing better after getting off to a bad 8–18 start. Finally, third baseman Robin Ventura, who sustained a broken ankle during spring training, was returning to the lineup. He, Frank Thomas, and Albert Belle made a solid 3–4–5 lineup. Maybe it was time to add a player or two as the trading deadline loomed? What were 3½ games, after all?

Section One—Overcoming History

But CEO Jerry Reinsdorf had a different view. He told a Chicago sportswriter, "Anyone who thinks we can catch Cleveland is crazy."[1] Like the 1994 strike, this only fueled more anger. Like Ozzie Guillén's "we don't owe the fans anything" soundbite two years earlier, these words would haunt Reinsdorf for a long time. In many ways, it still does over a quarter of a century later.

Wilson Álvarez, Danny Darwin, and Roberto Hernández were the three sent to the Giants. Álvarez would not have another big year in his career. Darwin retired after the 1998 season. Hernandez pitched for another 10 years and finish his career by appearing in 1,010 games. But the Sox gained reliever Keith Foulke, who was a big contributor in the 2000 division-winning season to compensate for losing closer Hernandez.

Yet this trade cannot be evaluated as most trades. This was not a simple matter of moving players back and forth. In the end, it did considerable damage to the franchise. In fact, it almost destroyed it.

The timing of the trade certainly was not good. It occurred only three years after the 1994 strike. Many fans were still convinced that Jerry Reinsdorf was not committed to winning. Furthermore, they thought, justly or unjustly, that Reinsdorf had been the driving force behind forcing the strike, and that he was more interested in breaking the players' union than taking his team to the World Series. And now this.

The Cleveland sports media went giddy, thinking the Indians now had a clear path to the division title. Cleveland did win the AL Central for the third straight time. However, they only had 86 wins, the lowest win total of their three AL division winners. Despite this, Cleveland went to and almost won the World Series. Only a one-run loss in Game 7 kept the Indians—now the Guardians—from a world championship.

And what about the White Sox in 1997? Even with the trade, they finished only six games behind Cleveland. Could they, like the team Jerry Reinsdorf said they couldn't catch, have gone to the World Series after a nearly 40-year absence? Of course, just as in 1994, that could not be known. The trade was a done deal.

Fan alienation deepened on the South Side of Chicago.

7. Backlash

Fast-forward to the home opener on April 9, 1999. There was a small dose of optimism as the season began. The Sox travelled to Seattle for three games. They won two, scoring 22 runs in the process. Good-hitting teams, even losing ones, can be entertaining. Besides, the Sox won their first series, and that had to be viewed as positive.

Chicago is known for its sometimes-harsh springs that often resemble winter. Some cynics thought the White Sox would always have some kind of attendance issue with many fans not wanting to sit in the spring cold to watch a game meant to be played in warm weather. Year after year, April games were a tough draw. But the conditions for the April 9 home opener were the worst I had ever experienced at either White Sox stadium. I felt frozen to my seat. Only 26,245 fans showed up. Had the awful weather chased away a walk-up crowd?

Perhaps, but the Opening Day attendance for the 1998 home opener had been slightly smaller. Even in years when expectations were low, the White Sox could always count on drawing 30,000 and more for their first home game of the season.

During the late 1990s, major league baseball had begun to recover from the effects of the 1994 strike, with the focus on the 1998 homer run chase by Mark McGwire and Sammy Sosa. That wasn't the case for the White Sox, at least not yet. Too much of a strike. Too much of a White Flag trade. Not enough of a World Series.

It didn't help that the White Sox played a bad game that Day in 1999. They committed five errors and lost to Kansas City, 10–5. Greg Norton played third base because Robin Ventura had been lost to free agency. Norton looked nervous any time the ball was hit to him, and he double-clutched even when making a routine throw to second for a force out. Norton made one of the five errors. (To be fair to Norton, he never claimed to be a third baseman, and he was asked to replace the excellent-fielding Ventura. Ventura would win six Gold Gloves in his career. Norton would not win any.)

It was amazing to see the Sox hit two home runs in that tundra. One came from Frank Thomas, which isn't all that amazing since the Hall of Famer could hit a home run any time in any condition. But

Section One—Overcoming History

the other homer came from a young player named Magglio Ordóñez. Ordóñez was in his second full season with the Sox. He had a powerful-looking swing, and that Opening Day homer was one of 30 he'd hit that season. Ordóñez was part of the late-decade rebuilding program. Perhaps the White Sox could be onto something after all.

Interleague play began in 1997. The first action between the White Sox and Cubs was at new Comiskey. The White Sox won two of three. They won game two on June 17 with a 5–3 victory. Roberto Hernández picked up a save despite giving up a run in the ninth. Wilson Álvarez threw a complete game shutout the next day giving the Sox a 3–0 win. In little more than a month later Hernandez and Álvarez were sent to San Francisco as part of the White Flag Trade.

In 1998, the White Sox were scheduled to travel across town to play the Cubs. If there was anything a Sox fan hated more than a strike or the White Flag Trade, it was losing to the Cubs. Regarding the three games against the Cubs, Sox fans had few expectations about their rebuilding team. Their team met these lowered expectations by getting swept. The first two games were competitive one-run affairs, but the Cubs finished the sweep by piling up 14 hits and winning, 13–7.

In 1999, Sox fans once again didn't look forward to their team returning to Wrigley Field. The Cubs had been a wild card team the year before and came into the series with a 32–24 record, in second place. Also, they had 66 home run-hitting Sammy Sosa. It looked like a possible sweep for the Cubs in their ivy-covered home field.

Four years later, I spoke with White Sox shortstop José Valentín how he felt about playing against the Cubs. He said two things. First, he didn't get as excited about the crosstown series as the fans did. He knew many of the players on the North Side. But he admitted that the games also got the competitive spirit going for him. "We wanted to show there were two baseball teams in Chicago," he told me.[2] (Since 1969, the White Sox had seemed like stepchildren in their own city.)

It was evident from the beginning that the 1999 series meant something to the Sox. When Ray Durham led off in game one, he

7. Backlash

didn't walk to the plate. He sprinted up to the box, showing he was anxious to play. He would get nine hits in the series.

And there was a sweep. An unanticipated White Sox sweep.

In game one, the Sox had a little luck. They won 5–3, but it was a rain shortened six inning contest. Some Sox fans sang as they walked out of Wrigley. Some Cubs fans threatened to beat the living crap out of them.

Game two was different. The Sox pounded out 18 hits and won, 8–2. The anxious Ray Durham picked up four of those 18 hits. The Cubs didn't score until the ninth inning, when the game was far out of reach.

Game three paid a small bit of justice to the White Flag Trade. Shortstop Mike Caruso had been a part of that trade, and he came up in the eighth inning with the game tied, 4–4 and a runner on. He sent a deep fly to right field. At first, it appeared that Sammy Sosa had a bead on it, but he stopped at the wall and helplessly watched it go into the seats above him. The White Sox completed their shocking sweep with a 6–4 win.

Finally, Sox fans felt they had something to celebrate. The decade was about to end, heading into a new millennium, and the team had only one playoff appearance in the last 16 years. As the rebuild slowly moved forward, it was still hard to know when the winning would begin. But now their team had swept the Cubs in the shrine known as Wrigley Field. One Sox fan posted on a fan website called whitesoxinteractve that he stuck a broom up through his T top and did a few laps around Wrigley. Yes, there was more than one baseball team in Chicago. As for the Cubs, they finished last in 1999.

Sox fans were encouraged by two other promising players developing. In his first full season, Paul Konerko hit 24 home runs with 81 RBI. Carlos Lee, another first-year player, posted power numbers of 16 home runs and 84 RBI, and he didn't start his season until May. Put these players in the lineup alongside Thomas, Durham, and Ordóñez, and the team began to take shape. Did the embittered fan base start noticing this potential?

Not right away, they didn't. In their next home game against Tampa Bay, slightly more than 15,000 fans showed up for a 9–7 Sox

Section One—Overcoming History

win. The Sox even beat up their former teammate, Wilson Álvarez of White Flag Trade fame, for eight runs. But radio play-by-play man John Rooney was frustrated by a crowd just over 15,000. Weren't the fans happy about the Cubs series?

Unfortunately for the White Sox, they played under .500 ball for the rest of the year. On August 13, they swept the Texas Ranger in a doubleheader in front of a decent but subdued crowd of 20,444. But they had slipped eight wins under .500. They finished in second place, but that was a deceptive result. The Sox ended up 21½ games behind Cleveland in a division that had only one team playing winning baseball. They had also won five fewer games than the year before.

How bad were things between the Sox franchise and its fans? Sports journalist Sridhar Pappu wrote a long piece for the *Chicago Reader*, a weekly newspaper. It appeared in early September. Pappu implored Jerry Reinsdorf to sell the team. He also quoted veteran *Tribune* sportswriter Bill Jauss about the White Sox situation. "It's as bad as I have ever seen it," Jauss said. "It's absolute apathy. It's like a relationship. If there's anger, at least there is emotion there. With time, nurture, and good luck, you can turn that emotion from hate to love. But if you're involved in a relationship where neither party gives a damn about the other, that's just about at the end of the road. I'm afraid this is where the Sox have come."[3]

The White Sox home attendance in 1998 and 1999 were the second lowest totals for the second White Sox stadium in any full season. The lowest occurred in the record setting during 121-loss season in 2024. The decade of the 1990s had begun with intense emotions and new optimism. It ended with a franchise in crisis.

8
◆ ◆ ◆
Overcoming Backlash

"The Kids Can Play" was a promotional slogan the White Sox used in 1999 and 2000. The team was selling the idea of a young ball club developing and eventually becoming a contending team. Even if fans didn't approve of the White Flag Trade, the idea of watching young players learn their trade had an appeal. For many fans, there was more charm in building a winner from the ground up rather than attempting to buy a pennant by purchasing big-time free agents with huge, long-term contracts. White Flag Trade or no White Flag Trade, the team had begun to assemble some promising young talent.

With second baseman Ray Durham at his side, manager Jerry Manuel spoke during a seminar at the SoxFest fan convention in January 2000. Manuel said it was time for his players to perform. He said he didn't want them hiding behind the fact that they were young. It was time to show their abilities, produce winning results, and leave the promotional slogans to someone else. Durham meekly remained silent.

For the most part, the fans attending Sox Fest that freezing January Saturday afternoon didn't expect much from the 2000 White Sox even if Jerry Manuel did. The team had only won 75 games the year before, and most didn't anticipate a serious run for a divisional title. It is doubtful the front office expected a big season, either. The only person who had high hopes was manager Jerry Manuel. So he began making demands of his team.

The White Sox decided to do something different for their home opener on April 14. For the first time in team history, the club played their first home game at night. This sounded risky considering the frigid conditions the year before, when hot chocolate sales outnumbered beer sales. In 1982, the Sox opener was postponed because of snow. A sign saying "No game today" stuck out of a snow drift in the middle of the infield. When the season finally did begin, the Sox got off to a hot 8–0 start even if their fans were still freezing their faces off.

Despite gambling with the weather, the scheduling made sense, at least to a point. Many fans would like to attend a home opener, but getting off work during the middle of the day can be tough. A night game was certainly more convenient.

The Sox began the season with a 10-game road trip in three different warm-weather cities. They posted a respectable 6–4 mark. The club also showed what kind of year it would be offensively when it scored 71 runs in this 10-game span.

Weather-wise, things worked out for this groundbreaking opener. April 14 was a beautiful spring night, almost feeling like summer. After drawing so poorly on the last two Opening Days, the team attracted 38,912 fans. Beer sales were up, and the stadium was loud.

Frank Thomas got things started in the first inning with his third home run of the young season, sending a drive into the right-center field seats. In inning two, Greg Norton, who had so much trouble in the 1999 opener, rocketed a double off the right-center field fence to bring in two. Perhaps Norton felt more comfortable at the plate knowing he was playing first base and not third.

Paul Konerko homered in the seventh inning. The Sox never trailed in the contest and won, 9–4. Yes, this team could hit. Maybe Jerry Manuel was right to expect big things from his players. They were kids no more. This was their best start since 1992.

In an afternoon home game on Saturday, April 22, the Sox and Tigers got into two ugly brawls. The first brawl began in the top of the seventh inning after Sox left-hander Jim Parque came in high and tight with a pitch, hitting Dean Palmer on the shoulder. (Carlos Lee had been hit by Tigers right hander Jeff Weaver in the bottom of the sixth, and Weaver had also hit Konerko in the fourth.)

Palmer charged the mound and threw his helmet. Both benches

8. Overcoming Backlash

and bullpens emptied, and chaos reigned as punches were thrown everywhere. Sox reliver Keith Foulke was sucker-punched in the face, and blood streamed down his uniform. From the White Sox, manager Manuel, Magglio Ordóñez, and Bill Simas were ejected. From the Tigers, Palmer, backup catcher Robert Fick, and Danny Patterson were also thrown out. For some reason, Fick returned to the Tigers' bullpen and taunted fans. The fans doused him with beer, and he seemed to thrive in the moment. The beer kept coming, and he stood there and got drenched, holding his arms up in defiance. Things were not over.

In the top of the ninth inning, Sox reliever Tanyon Sturtze hit Deivi Cruz. Sturtze was ejected. Then Bobby Howry hit Shane Halter, and another brawl ensued. Dean Palmer came out of the Tigers' clubhouse to join the melee even though he had already been thrown out of the game.

All in all, 16 players would be suspended for a combined total of 82 games. Manuel and Tigers manager Phil Garner were suspended for eight games each. Keith Foulke got five stitches in his face.

Oh, and who won the game? The White Sox truly put the game away in the eighth inning with home runs by Konerko and Chris Singleton, winning 14–4. They piled up 14 hits in another impressive offensive performance. The next day, they finished the three-game sweep with a 9–4 victory. In the three-game weekend series, the Sox scored 30 runs.

The struggling Tigers left Chicago with a 4–13 record, and there was the usual theory that a brawl could be a unifying force for a losing team. The Tigers eventually improved their play, but the White Sox still won the head-to-head series, 9–3. Detroit finished the season four wins under .500, 16 games behind the Sox.

By the end of April, the White Sox were 17–8. After beating the Cubs two of three in early June, their record improved to 37–24. They stood in first place, two games ahead of Cleveland. But was this team as good as their record indicated? So far, they were playing up to Jerry Manuel's expectations, but was this team for real? Was the rebuilding program supposed to work this fast?

A challenging road test awaited them. There were three games

Section One—Overcoming History

in Cleveland and four in New York. The Indians and Yankees had dominated the American League during the second half of the 1990s, going to five World Series between them. Most Sox fans thought a 4–3 trip would be a good showing.

The Sox began by winning two one-run decisions in Cleveland. They finished the sweep by romping over the Indians, 11–4. The team then produced even more offense against the Yankees.

The Sox continued their offensive assault by pounding New York, 12–3, in game one. They knocked out 16 hits and chased talented Yankees left-hander Andy Pettitte. The Sox scored in every one of the last six innings.

In the second game, the Sox were held to three runs but still came out victorious, 3–1. James Baldwin improved his record to 10–1. Reliever Bobby Howry, who came to the Sox in the White Flag Trade, got the final five outs.

The Yankees played more like the defending world champions that they were in game three. Down 10–3, New York came back and trailed by only one run in the bottom of the ninth. Third baseman Scott Brosius represented the winning run at the plate with two outs, but he grounded out to third. Keith Foulke, another picked up from the White Flag Trade, notched his 16th save as he had become the team's closer.

Then came the massacre in the series finale. The Sox sent 12 men to the plate in the first inning. The rally was capped off by a grand slam hit by José Valentín. Valentín's drive sailed way over the 385-foot marker in right-center. The poor defending world champion Yankees hadn't even come to bat yet, but they trailed, 9–0.

It was the first time since 1962 that the Sox scored nine runs in the first inning. Even though it was only mid–June, according to TV play-by-play man Ken Harrelson, they had batted around in an inning for the 14th time in 2000.

Yankees fans were more angry at their team than impressed by the White Sox. Many of the 52,856 in Yankee Stadium booed their champions. More boos cascaded down in the second inning as the Sox added three more runs. One small consolation for Yankees fans was that the Sox didn't bat around again, although they did come

8. Overcoming Backlash

close. But the game was humiliating enough for New York. The Sox won, 17–4, as they amassed 18 hits.

During this season-defining, seven-game road trip, Chicago outscored Cleveland and New York by a combined 65–31. The 1977 White Sox, known as the South Side Hitmen, had excited their fans with a powerful offense, but they had done nothing like this. In fact, in a role reversal, the 2000 Sox looked like the powerful Yankees teams of the 1950s and early 1960s.

The White Sox strengthened their hold on first place as their record rose to 20 wins over .500. A homecoming occurred on Monday, June 19, and Sox fans were there to greet them. *Many* Sox fans were there to greet them.

The streets around Comiskey Park II were jammed with a massive walk-up crowd. One would have thought the World Series had come to the South Side of Chicago. Three years later, fan Matt Cianchetti told me of his experience that night.

> I went online the Sunday night before the game and purchased two tickets which to my surprise were all the way in the 500 level of the upper deck. As most Sox fans would know, this would be unheard-of for our team to be this close to a sellout on a weekday night. We knew it was going to be a jacked-up crowd, and that we would have to leave early. We ended up leaving early, but still got snarled up in a standstill traffic jam on the Kennedy Expressway anyway. The source of this huge traffic jam? The Thirty-First and Thirty-Fifth Street exits to Comiskey Park. Traffic was backed up all the way to the Loop.
>
> By the time we got to the ballpark exits, it was already in the fourth inning. All the parking lots were sold out, and there were thousands milling around the ballpark looking for tickets. At this point, we decided to cut our losses on the upper deck seats and call it a night. We took the rest of the game in at a local bar.
>
> We later heard on the radio that the game was a complete sellout, and the reason the parking lots were sold out was that an estimated 56,000 [people] had descended on the ballpark. Maybe they just thought they could park and go up to the ticket window to buy tickets [only] to find out the game was sold out completely. Not to mention they blocked people who had tickets from getting in.[1]

The White Sox won the game, 6–1, before an announced crowd of 43,062. Cianchetti never got any closer than a bar stool, looking up at a television. Despite this, he wasn't overly disappointed. "Even

Section One—Overcoming History

though I was disappointed that I couldn't make it into the ballpark," he said, "I was happy White Sox fever was gripping Chicago. It was the most unforgettable game I never made it to."[2]

Where a team stands at the beginning of September is a solid indicator of the chances that team has of winning its division. Going into that critical month, the White Sox stood in first place, 7½ games ahead of second-place Cleveland. The Anaheim Angels came into Chicago for a three-game weekend series.

Trailing 8–3 in the bottom of the eighth inning in game one, the Sox rallied for six runs on the strength of back-to-back home runs by Thomas and Ordóñez. Keith Foulke closed it out in the ninth for his 26th save of the season. The Angels had to feel frustrated. They scored eight runs on 10 hits and hit two homers, and they lost. But after all, the Sox racked up 14 hits and slugged three homers.

The hitting continued for both sides, but the Sox prevailed in the next two games as well, 13–6 and 13–12. Chicago outscored Anaheim, 35–26, in a three-game slugfest. Yes, the Angels scored 26 runs in three games and *still* got swept.

Cleveland had to feel frustrated, too. They won two out of three in their weekend series, yet they lost ground. Their five-year streak of division titles was coming to an end.

The 1977 South Side Hitmen had excited their fans as they slugged their way to 90 wins. But that team lacked depth, slumped badly in August, and ended up 12 games behind first-place Kansas City. They just didn't accomplish what the 2000 club did.

In 2000, the White Sox set a franchise record with 978 runs scored—the most in 64 years. That total was also the best in the majors in 2000. Combined, Frank Thomas and Magglio Ordóñez drove in 269 runs. In addition, the Sox had three other players who drove in over 90 runs. The team scored in double figures 28 times and hit 216 home runs. There was no late-season slump for them.

The White Sox clinched their title in an anti-climactic fashion. They had a five-game winning streak broken on September 24 when they lost to the Twins, 6–5, in Minnesota. But the Indians had lost, 9–0, to Kansas City, so the White Sox had won the AL Central for the first time since they had won the old AL West seven years prior.

8. Overcoming Backlash

In reality, winning the division was never in doubt even though this was their first winning season in four years.

There was a game in Cleveland the next day, and Indians players showed some class by congratulating the White Sox players. Now it was on to the post-season.

The opponent in the three-of-five Divisional Series was the wild card Seattle Mariners. Seattle had won 91 games during the regular season, and an eight-game winning streak in September had helped them get into the post-season. Like the White Sox, they were a good offensive club and had scored 907 runs. They hit 198 home runs. In the second-to-last game of the season, the Mariners had rung up 21 runs on 22 hits. They had an aging but still good Rickey Henderson, Edgar Martínez, John Olerud, and Jay Buhner. They also had Alex Rodriguez right before he signed his quarter-of-a-billion-dollar contract with Texas. This would be a challenging series.

The first inning of Game 1 was a strange one for the White Sox. Rickey Henderson led off and hit a ground ball to the right side of the infield. For some reason, second baseman Ray Durham was edging toward the middle of the infield, and Henderson's ground ball rolled through Durham's vacated spot for a single.

Jim Parque was on the mound, and of course, he was concerned about Henderson stealing second. The distracted Parque hit Mike Cameron with a pitch. Alex Rodriguez was next, and he hit a soft single to right, scoring Henderson. Parque had made a good pitch, getting in on Rodriguez's hands, but Rodriguez was able to muscle the ball to the outfield. Seattle had men on first and third with no outs. It looked like they could break open Game 1 right in the first inning.

Edgar Martínez lined out to shortstop José Valentín, who made a leaping catch of a softly hit ball. John Olerud bounced a grounder up the middle. Durham made a diving grab and made an acrobatic flip to Valentín for the force at second. But Valentín's relay to first was not in time to complete the double play, and Cameron scored. The inning finished with Seattle leading, 2–0.

But should Seattle have scored at all? The Mariners never hit the ball with any authority. It was a strange inning that should have ended with no runs scored. And it was an indicator of stranger things to come, not only in this game, but throughout the series.

In the bottom of the third inning, the Sox took a 4–3 lead when Durham hit an opposite-field homer to left-center, and Ordóñez tripled in Valentín. The Mariners tied it in the seventh, and the game went into extra innings. The top of the 10th was almost as strange as the top of the first.

Mike Cameron singled to lead off the inning. He stayed at first when Rodriguez flied to left. Then Sox reliever Keith Foulke became distracted by the speedy Cameron. He threw over to first base five times. Mariners manager Lou Pinella called time and went out to speak to Cameron. It looked like an involved discussion.

Cameron ran on the next pitch. Sox catcher Josh Paul made a good throw, but Cameron was safe on a close play. Durham argued that Cameron's hand had come off the bag, but the second base umpire disagreed. The go-ahead run was on second, which had been Foulke's biggest fear.

But Foulke should have been more concerned about Edgar Martínez, who had hit 37 homers in the 2000 season. Martínez launched a drive to left field for a two-run homer. John Olerud made things worse by hitting a homer to right-center. The Mariners led, 7–4, and won by that score.

Because White Sox pitchers had become too distracted with base stealers, Seattle was able to pick up five runs. The Sox could have and should have won this game. But could haves and should haves don't count for much.

In Game 2, the White Sox scored right way when Durham and Valentine doubled in the first inning. Valentín stole third, and it looked like the Sox would have a multi-run inning. It didn't happen, though, as Valentín was stranded at third when Thomas, Carlos Lee, and Konerko failed to bring him home.

The Sox could only pick up three hits during the rest of the game. Seattle took a 2–0 Series lead, winning 5–2. For the White Sox, it was their ninth post-season loss at home in a row. The only post-season win at home since 1919 had been in 1959, when they won the first game of the World Series, 11–0, against the Dodgers. Ted

8. Overcoming Backlash

Kluszewski hit two homers in that game, and old, nasty Early Wynn pitched seven shutout innings.

Elimination came in the next game in Seattle as the White Sox managed only one run on three hits. But a case can be made that the Sox could have won this game or at least should have had another chance to win it.

The game was tied, 1–1, in the bottom of the ninth inning. John Olerud led off with an infield single and advanced to second on a throwing error by pitcher Kelly Wunsch. Foulke replaced Wunsch on the mound. Rickey Henderson ran for Olerud and advanced to third on a Stan Javier bunt.

On the verge of elimination, the White Sox brought their infield and outfield in. Carlos Guillén laid down a perfect bunt that got past first baseman Konerko. Henderson scored with ease. Game, series, and season were over.

But wait a minute. Guillén should have been called out. He had stepped on home plate as he put down his bunt. Rules state simply that a hitter cannot leave the box when making contact. Henderson should have been sent back to third, and the Sox would have had a chance to get out of the inning by retiring the next hitter, Mark McLemore. Maybe they could have won in extra innings and maybe the next two games. But the Mariners were allowed to celebrate a win in a game that should have continued.

It felt like 1983 all over again. A team that hit .286 in the regular season managed but seven runs in three games. This came from a squad that scored nine runs in the first inning twice during the regular season.

It was reported that owners Jerry Reinsdorf and Eddie Einhorn blankly stared ahead as they rode in an elevator. The loss had to be especially disappointing for Reinsdorf, as he had felt vindicated for the White Flag Trade. The fan backlash had been intense.

But this was a young, talented team that now had playoff experience. There was always next season, right? Well, no.

9
♦ ♦ ♦

The Wells Season

In late January 2001, at SoxFest, new White Sox GM Kenny Williams said, "We needed an ace, and the price for an ace is high. We won 95 games and got to the playoffs, and that wasn't enough."

What was Williams referring to as he spoke at SoxFest? He had just made a multi-player trade to Toronto that was essentially a lefty for lefty deal. The Sox sent the young Mike Sirotka to the Blue Jays and got a guy who had been around the block, David Wells, 37. Sirotka, 29, had won 15 games in 2000. Wells was a 20-game winner that year. In effect, this was the opposite of the White Flag trade where a younger player was sent away, and the future was now. Williams was sending a strong message to the fans that he was going for it.

The most important thing for Williams was that Wells was a proven performer in the post-season with an 8–1 record. In Williams' mind, Wells was the bridge to the World Series.

Wells did come with a little baggage, though. He used two words to describe Blue Jays fans: "stink" and "terrible." Jays GM Gord Ash denied that controversy regarding the fans was the motivation behind the trade, even though he thought Wells' comments "were uncalled for."

"It [the Wells controversy] did not play a role in this transaction," Ash said. "It was a baseball transaction, first and foremost. He was an important guy for us, but it was time for him to move on."[1]

Regardless of any controversy in Toronto, Kenny Williams was a big admirer of Wells. "He leads by example on the field," Williams said. "Off the field, he's his own man. He always has been."[2]

9. The Wells Season

The White Sox would find out how Wells was going to be his own man.

Speaking at SoxFest, Williams said he had warned the Blue Jays about some arm problems Sirotka had. He added that he had provided medical information about Sirotka, and that they, the Blue Jays, would have to "shut him down" at times. Otherwise, the optimistic Williams looked forward to what he thought would be a landmark season.

But all was not well. When Sirotka arrived for spring training, the Jays found that he had a torn labrum. Toronto GM Ash cried foul, saying he had been tricked, and appealed to Baseball Commissioner Bud Selig to overturn the trade. Kenny Williams cried foul himself, saying that he had been transparent and that he didn't appreciate Ash's accusations. After all, what other GM would want to deal with Williams if he had the reputation of a con artist?[3]

Selig ruled in favor of the White Sox and Williams. "After careful consideration of all the information before me, I uphold the transaction and deny the Toronto club's claim for relief," Selig said. "Although there is a dispute about whether certain facts about Sirotka's condition were disclosed before the clubs agreed to the trade, the Toronto club spoke directly to Sirotka about his health on the day of the trade and believed it had the opportunity to make the trade conditional. The Blue Jays never elected to do so."[4]

Not a great endorsement of Williams, but the trade was upheld. In the long run, this trade was a disaster for almost everyone. Only Williams came out relatively unscathed.

Mike Sirotka never pitched an inning for Toronto. Sadly for him, he would never pitch another inning for anyone. His career ended with Toronto. Gordon Ash's career with Toronto ended, too. He was fired at the end of the 2001 season as the Blue Jays finished 16 games behind the first-place Yankees.

In the 2001 White Sox season opener at Cleveland, everything went as Williams dreamed it would. Wells pitched six strong innings, giving up two runs on four hits. Magglio Ordóñez homered, and Keith Foulke picked up the save in a 7–4 White Sox win.

Section One—Overcoming History

It seemed like 2000 all over again. Maybe this time a World Series would happen.

But things soon went sour. The White Sox suffered through four early four-game losing streaks, with Wells losing three of four decisions. By early May, the team stood at 8–18. The White Sox sat in last place, already 11 games out. Spring seemed very cold in Chicago, as cold as that Opening Day in 1999.

But there was an even worse crisis looming. Playing first base on April 27, Frank Thomas dove for a ball and hurt his right arm. He was taken out of the game, and days later he still couldn't swing a bat. He remained out of action.

In the meantime, David Wells had gotten a part-time gig on Chicago radio station WMVP-AM 1000. He decided to sound off on the Thomas situation, as he didn't believe the Thomas injury was a serious one. "If you don't have the guts to be out there, you don't need to be here," Wells said on WMVP. "Playing hurt will get you a lot more respect from your fellow players."

Yes, that was David Wells being his own man again.

A week later, the White Sox announced that Thomas had a strained right triceps and was out for the season. Surgery awaited him. "I've been doubted my whole life as a professional athlete, or as an athlete period," Thomas said regarding the Wells controversy. "It doesn't bother me. I know what I'm made of. It's character-building. People don't know what makes me tick. I've done a lot in this game, and I hope to continue to do a lot. Just got to do a lot. Just going to have a little break here and get my arm together and be ready to play next year."[5]

Meanwhile, the David Wells situation continued to not pay off for the White Sox.

In a June 8 home game against the Cubs, Wells faced five batters in the first inning and got none of them out. He made two errors, including a throw that sailed down the right field line. He left the game with back spasms. He'd make a few more starts, but essentially his season was over in June. Wells ended up with five wins. The only thing that could be said in his favor was that he had five more wins than Mike Sirotka.

9. The Wells Season

Despite all of this, the White Sox had recovered enough to win 83 games and finished only eight games behind Cleveland. It was at least possible that they could have won the division with a healthy David Wells and Frank Thomas. But like 1994, that cannot really be known. All that is known for certain is that the Wells acquisition didn't work out so well, and he would move on once more. Still, it must be said the offense still hit 214 home runs with Frank Thomas gone most of the season.

But there was a young left-handed pitcher who had a stellar season in his first full year. His record was 16–8 with a 3.29 ERA. His strikeout-walk ratio was 126–48. He gave up 188 hits in 221⅓ innings. He didn't waste time pitching. He'd get the ball and throw it. Sox fans could relax when he was on the mound because the opposition usually went down meekly, and the inning would be over in about five minutes. His name was Mark Buehrle.

10

♦ ♦ ♦

Us vs. Them

There has been a long-standing rivalry between the White Sox and the Cubs, and it was there well before interleague play started. Many long-time fans love one team and won't even tolerate the other. Loyalty to a team usually was passed down through the generations.

When interleague play began, White Sox-Cubs games were often described as being like playoff games. The games had importance since they counted in the standings, but they didn't have the significance of a playoff game. Yet the emotions of these games were raw.

I attended a Sox-Cubs game at Wrigley on July 7, 2000. From the first pitch on, the atmosphere was intense. Cubs fans celebrated when Kerry Wood got Frank Thomas looking at strike three in the sixth inning. Sox fans celebrated when their team won in extra innings. While some players were puzzled by this fanaticism, they had to be affected by the noise, the emotion, the electricity. That July game did seem like a playoff game with inflated importance.

In 2004, the White Sox ran a TV commercial that capsulated the rivalry from the South Side viewpoint. It can be described as controversial and effective. With the "1812 Overture" playing in the background, it went like this:

> **VOICE:** The White Sox present a comparison
> **THEM VS. US**
> **THEY:** Are lovable when they lose
> **US:** We hate losing
> **THEY:** Champions in 1908
> **US:** Champions as recently as 1917
> **THEY:** Believe they're cursed

10. Us vs. Them

Us: Agree
They: Got Wood
We: Got Lumber
They: Have a fan who says "Woo"
We: Don't

White Sox fans embraced the message of this commercial, and Brooks Boyer, the Sox marketing man responsible for the ad, instantly became a cult hero. The commercial spoke directly to the team's fan base, which was important after the friction caused by the 1994 strike and the 1997 White Flag Trade. Since Jerry Reinsdorf, the man with the memories of the Brooklyn Dodgers, was sometimes thought of as not understanding Chicago baseball history, this touching of the emotions of the Sox fan base was a breakthrough in the still-troubled fan-franchise relations.

Most of the references were obvious. The "Got Wood" reference was to Cubs pitcher Kerry Wood. Wood was a talented but injury-ridden player. He did strike out 20 Astros in a 1998 game where he barely missed getting a no-hitter. The lumber referred to the potent White Sox offense.

The reference about a fan saying "woo" was aimed at Cubs fan named Ronnie "Woo-Woo" Wickers, who went around yelling "woo-woo" at Wrigley Field or just about anywhere. Cubs fans loved him; Sox fans couldn't stand him. I saw him at a SoxFest wearing a Cubs hat and warmup jacket. He was there to attract attention and taunt. I turned my back and pretended not to see him.

Cubs fans and the Cubs-loving Chicago sports media whined about the ad picking on the poor Cubs, but Boyer defended himself. "We're not taking shots at the Cubs," Boyer told the *Tribune*. "That's clearly not our intention. We're really passionate about our team."

"At the same time, this is sports, and we like to have fun with some of our ads."[1]

Boyer wasn't acting defensive because there was no need. When a politician runs for a nomination for an office, he/she has to appeal to the party base first. They are not going to worry about offending the opposition until later. This ad must be considered one of the most effective of its kind. It directly appealed to its fan base, and it didn't

Section One—Overcoming History

matter if Cubs fans and their friends in the media suffered from hurt feelings.

While this advertisement ran in June 2004 right around scheduled games against the Cubs, the White Sox-Cubs rivalry was a motivating factor in making moves to make a run at the division in 2003.

It was June 20, 2003, and the White Sox were a disappointing six wins under .500. They were set to begin a three-game series against the Cubs at Wrigley Field. Another three-game series would follow a week later at the Sox venue that was now called U.S. Cellular Field.

The White Sox won four of the six games. They excited their fans with two walk-offs at U.S. Cellular. José Valentín homered for one win. D'Angelo Jiménez singled in Magglio Ordóñez for the other victory.

After beating the Cubs, the White Sox were still three wins under .500. Yet they were only 4½ games out of first place. Maybe they weren't so bad after all? To fortify the team, GM Kenny Williams traded for Carl Everett and Roberto Alomar two days after the second series ended.

In late July, the Sox won 13 out of 14 games. They were in a virtual tie for first with Kansas City with the Twins in fourth four games out.

Toward the end of August, the Sox travelled to New York to play the Yankees. The Sox won two of three games in the same manner as the beating they gave the Yankees in 2000. In the first game, the Sox slammed four home runs off Roger Clemens in a 13–2 win. The next night, they beat up on old nemesis David Wells by pounding him for 10 runs and 11 hits in 5⅓ innings. Frank Thomas had to take some pleasure when he homered off Wells in the fourth inning.

"They just pummeled us," Yankees manager Joe Torre said to ESPN after the game.

Pummeled was an apt description. The White Sox were now in first place by themselves.

By early September, the Twins had now become the biggest rival. On September 8, they came into Chicago for a four-games series with the teams tied.

In game one, the White Sox scored five runs in the first inning,

10. Us vs. Them

and the Twins answered with two runs in the second. That was it for the scoring as Bartolo Colon threw a complete game for the Sox for his 13th win.

In game two, the Sox hit three homers and led, 8–2, going to the ninth inning. So far, they had outscored the Twins, 13–4, in the series, and it appeared they had all the momentum. But then came the ninth....

José Paniagua was a right-handed relief pitcher who had bounced around the major leagues since 1996. The Sox picked him up at the end of August, and he was making his first appearance. His job was just to get the Twins out in the ninth and wrap up a game without the Sox having to use to their closer. That didn't happen.

Paniagua gave up three hits and a walk. Manuel had seen enough and called for closer Tom Gordon. Before Paniagua left, however, he got into an argument with home plate umpire Mark Carlson. Carlson threw Paniagua out of the game, and Paniagua made obscene gestures before he left the field. With two outs, Michael Cuddyer was at the plate representing the tying run. Gordon struck him out to end the game. The White Sox won, but a blowout had turned into a slim 8–6 win. As for Paniagua, the White Sox released him the next day, and he never pitched in the major leagues again.

Did that four-run rally in the ninth do something for the Twins? It seemed so as Minnesota won games three and four, 4–1 and 5–2. In the last game, Twins starter Brad Radke threw a complete game, beating Sox pitcher Esteban Loaiza, who was going for his 20th win. The Twins and Sox were tied for first place again.

A week later, the scene shifted to Minneapolis for a three-game series. The Sox went into the series a half-game out.

Game one was a disaster for the Sox. Loaiza was trying again for his 20th win but had been sick before the game. He even told Sox radio color man Ed Farmer that there was a possibility he would throw up on the mound. It didn't take long for him to work up a sweat. In 2⅓ innings, he threw 74 pitches and walked five hitters. The Twins built up a 4–0 lead and won, 5–2. Brad Radke beat the Sox again, this time going seven innings. Carl Everett hit a ninth-inning home run, but no one was on base, so the hit was meaningless.

Section One—Overcoming History

So why did manager Jerry Manuel let a sick Loaiza pitch? "He was a little under the weather," Manuel admitted. "But you don't sit nobody because of a cough. It's the major leagues. You have to be ready to perform."[2]

But it didn't look like Loaiza was ready to perform. His macho act didn't work, and the White Sox had now lost three straight to the Twins. Make that four straight. The Twins won game two, 4–2. The Sox didn't score until the seventh inning, when Joe Crede hit a two-run homer. Eddie Guardado recorded his 37th save for the Twins.

The Sox finally got their first lead of the series by scoring two runs in the first inning in game three. But that didn't last the inning, as the Twins responded with two runs of their own. The nearly 40,000 Twins fans cheered with delight as their team completed the sweep with a 5–3 win.

For the White Sox, the season was over. Loaiza finally got number 20 by beating the Yankees a week later, but by that time the Twins had clinched the division. Minnesota finished four games ahead of the Sox. The loud cheers from the Metrodome probably still rang in their ears.

What happened to the contending Sox that they lost one game after another to the Twins? At least one observer said the Twins did more when it came to playing fundamental baseball. "We have a lot of guys who do the little things," Twins catcher A.J. Pierzynski told *Tribune* columnist Rick Morrissey. "We have guys who will bunt. We've got guys who will steal bases."[3]

Sounds like the 2005 White Sox, doesn't it? Pierzynski had a great deal of praise for the Sox, though some of it had to be backhanded.

> The middle of their lineup is as good as it gets. Carlos Lee is having a year I always knew he was capable of. Frank Thomas is having another Frank year. Magglio Ordóñez is having his standard year … 320, 30 homers, and 100 RBIs. We don't have those guys. We have Torii [Hunter] and we have Torii.
>
> Esteban Loaiza has a chance to win the Cy Young. Bartolo Colon is a very good pitcher. I hate facing him. I hate facing Buehrle. I hate facing Loaiza. I can't hit Loaiza to save my life. And their bullpen. Marte is one of the best left-handed relievers in the league. Tom Gordon is probably the nastiest pitcher I faced all year.[4]

10. Us vs. Them

A great deal of praise, but according to columnist Morrissey, it didn't amount to much. "There are lessons in all of this," he wrote, "but it will take time to sort them out. You get the feeling the Twins would be willing to go through a wall for each other. You get the feeling the Sox would look at the wall, then at each other, and then decide for a ladder."[5]

On the other side of town, the Cubs won the NL Central Division. They beat the 101-win Atlanta Braves in the Division Series in five games. Kerry Wood dominated the Braves in the deciding Game 5 when he gave up one run in eight innings. It looked like the Cubs were heading to the World Series when they took a three-games-to-one lead against the Marlins in the NLCS. But they blew that lead and stretched their streak of not winning a World Series to 95 years.

It should have been an all–Chicago World Series. But the Cubs couldn't overcome the so-called Bartman Game. And the White Sox got no help from Jose Paniagua. It was a typical Chicago baseball ending.

Who would have won this all–Chicago series? Each team had talent. A Chicago team had to be the winner. Both Chicago teams couldn't have blown it even if they tried. What kind of commercial could Brooks Boyer have run if the White Sox had won it? Would there have been anything left of the city no matter who won?

But the White Sox sat out the playoffs once again. In a column published on September 18, *Tribune* writer Phil Rogers predicted an end to Manuel's career as White Sox manager. "Manuel, it seems, always has had a huge personnel edge over the Twins," Rogers wrote. "Yet in these last three seasons, Tom Kelly and Ron Gardenhire [Twins managers] have produced a 262–213 record in Minnesota. Manuel has the Sox at 244–231. That's an 18-game edge for the franchise with inferior talent."[6]

Rogers' column had a "No postseason, no Manuel" headline. White Sox management agreed. Jerry Manuel was fired at the end of the season, as winning 86 games was looked upon as true under-achieving. The franchise replaced Manuel with Ozzie Guillén.

How would have team history had changed if the White Sox had at least won the AL Central? Of course, that can't be known.

85

Section One—Overcoming History

However, the team rebuilding that had begun with the White Flag Trade in 1997 was nearing an end with one division title and no post-season wins. Their own streak of not winning a World Series was pushing 90 years. Things would have to change. Decisions would have to be made. Either that or a frustrated fan base would be convinced that the organization wasn't serious about winning anything.

11

♦ ♦ ♦

Ozzie Guillén
Player and Then Manager

Ozzie Guillén's long association with the Chicago White Sox began on December 6, 1984, when the team acquired him from the San Diego Padres. The Sox sent LaMarr Hoyt, Kevin Kerstein and Todd Simmons to the Padres for Guillén, Tim Lollar, Bill Long, and Luis Salazar. There are many names there, but most looked at this as a Hoyt for Guillén trade.

Initial reaction from Sox fans was not good, or at the very least, skeptical. Right-handed pitcher Hoyt was only one season away from his Cy Young Award year. Trading an ace for a rookie shortstop? The only White Sox pitcher to win a playoff game in a quarter of a century? And who was this Ozzie Guillén anyway?

Guillén was part of a long line of shortstops from Venezuela for the White Sox. Chico Carrasquel played for the club from 1950 to 1955. Carrasquel put in a 10-year career and picked up 1,199 hits. The next year, Luis Aparicio took over the short- stop position as a rookie. He won the 1956 Rookie of the Year Award in the American League. He had two stints with the White Sox, beginning with 1956–1962 and later 1968–1970. Aparicio won nine Gold Gloves. He was inducted into the Hall of Fame in 1984.

Would Guillén rate with either one of these shortstops? He did at least in 1985, when he was named American League Rookie of the Year.

Guillén will forever be associated with the 1990 White Sox squad. Despite not having a 20-game winner or a hitter with 20

Section One—Overcoming History

home runs, the 1990 Sox won 94 games, good for third best in Major League Baseball. (And one win behind second-best Atlanta.) It was also a whopping 25-game improvement over the 1989 team that lost 92 games and ended up last in the AL West.

The 1990 season was also the last at Comiskey Park after an 80-year run. The Sox won the last home game in typical 1990 fashion by beating Seattle, 2–1. With the game tied, 1–1 in the bottom of the sixth inning, Frank Thomas stood at first base after an RBI single. Left-handed Dan Pasqua went to the opposite field with what looked like another single. But the ball took a tricky hop past Ken Griffey, Sr. and rolled to the wall. Thomas scored as Pasqua picked up a lucky triple. The one-run lead held up as reliever Bobby Thigpen earned one of his then-record 57 saves.

At the game's end, fans tearfully said goodbye to the old ballpark. With the team's 1990 turnaround, attendance had increased by almost a million from the previous season. It eclipsed the 2,000,000 mark for the first time in six years. Fans fondly remembered the club for "doing the little things." Guillén was looked at as a veteran leader of the beloved team.

Guillén was a fun-loving player. In a home game in early April 1991, Tigers manager Sparky Anderson had Guillén intentionally walked in the eighth inning. On getting to first base, Guillén turned and playfully goaded Anderson as he sat in the first base dugout. Anderson responded with an equally playful thumbing of the nose at Guillén.

Guillén also built the reputation of being outspoken and not minding offending people with his opinions. However, there was one time his comments were misunderstood, and White Sox fans turned on him. At that time, his past popularity didn't seem to matter.

On August 10, 1994, the White Sox held onto first place in the newly created American League Central Division. They led Cleveland by only one game, and third-place Kansas City was only four games behind. The division title wasn't a given, but the Sox had a sterling rotation, and they had to be considered the team to beat. In addition, 1994 introduced the wild card playoff system, and it was thought by many that the White Sox would get into the playoffs one way or another.

11. Ozzie Guillén

Of course, the strike ended all of that. For the first time since 1903, there was no World Series or post-season of any kind. Would the White Sox finally have made another World Series appearance after a 35-year absence? Fans were embittered because there was no way to answer that question.

The White Sox finally returned to the field on April 26, 1995, after the work stoppage ended. They lost their first four games by a combined score of 39–11. Their record quickly dropped to 2–8. This was the team that was supposed to go to the World Series? Oh, yes, the World Series that never happened in 1994 and hadn't happened in Chicago since 1959.

Though they shouldn't have been surprised, players and owners were caught off guard and stung by the intense fan anger. It is hard to come up with a consensus of who the fans truly held responsible for the 1994–1995 work stoppage. In the end, it made no real difference. Baseball had been stopped in August 1994, and, in the end, it was a pox on both houses.

Suddenly in early May, there was a startling headline in the *Chicago Sun-Times*. "We don't owe the fans anything," it read. The person making this utterance? The fun-loving fan favorite Ozzie Guillén.

From a public relations viewpoint, at least on the surface, there couldn't have been a dumber thing to say. This was no time to lash out at the fans, especially when their bitterness was so intense and fresh. And this was no time for a White Sox player to pick a fight with fans when the team was playing so badly.

In the fast-moving media world, sound-bite statements like this have a great deal of power. The context in which it was said often makes no difference. Whether the players owe fans anything is debatable, but regardless, Ozzie Guillén appeared arrogant and insensitive. Fans were not going to forget this quote. They still haven't forgotten it almost three decades later; it is something that lives on even though it is not fully understood.

I interviewed Guillén for my first book back in the spring of 1999 and asked him about that statement. I thought he would get angry or defensive. Instead, he welcomed the question. He was proud of what he had said. As he put it in context, he should have been proud. "I said that to the fans because I saw them call Frank Thomas a nigger," Guillén told me. "We don't owe them anything. They were calling Frank names, and he was upset about it. He wasn't upset; he was sad. If they [the fans] don't want to come, don't. If you do come, don't treat people like that. That happened in Toronto. In Toronto, they were calling us all kinds of names for no reason."[1]

Guillén said he went on the radio and vented. He realized that some fans were upset about Thomas having a home built with non-union help while the players were on strike. But he thought they went way too far, especially with the racist name-calling.

"That's why I did it, and I don't regret it," Guillén said. "It's not because of the fans, it was because of what people were doing. There's no one who appreciated the fans in Chicago more than Ozzie Guillén. I treat the fans the way they should be treated. I love my fans. They showed up at the last game I played for the White Sox."[2] (That was on September 27, 1997, against Kansas City.)

Guillén still takes some heat for the "we don't owe the fans anything" comment. However, the story behind this memorable line has long been forgotten or not even known. Yet Guillén was able and willing to handle a public controversy and stand by his beliefs. Isn't that quality helpful for a major league manager?

During his interview with me, he talked about the White Sox in glowing terms. He had told *Tribune* reporter Phil Rogers about his unhappiness about the White Sox not picking up his contract in 1998. But Rogers wrote that Guillén also said he wanted to work in some capacity with the White Sox once his playing days were over.[3]

I am convinced that one reason Guillén agreed to be interviewed by me was that he wanted to campaign for the White Sox manager's job. I am not a celebrity media person by any means, but the written word has power to it. In looking back at his time with White Sox during his talk with me, he spoke of the good times, praised Jerry Reinsdorf, and remembered the 1990 Sox team that won 94 games with great fondness. However, I am also certain he just wanted to talk and was happy someone wanted to listen. (However, Guillén didn't respond to an interview request for this book.)

11. Ozzie Guillén

A little more than four years later, he was named manager of the Chicago White Sox. He would win a World Series, still the only White Sox manager to do so since Pants Rowland in 1917. He would earn great praise. He would again be involved in more controversy. And, no matter what people thought of him, he will always be remembered, maybe even more so than the team he played on and managed.

Section Two

Making History

The previous part of this story was about a team that had some success, but somehow found ways not to achieve something significant that seemed within their grasp. Here is a list of players on the White Sox roster one time or another from 1990 to 2004: Carlton Fisk, Frank Thomas, Robin Ventura, Jack McDowell, Sammy Sosa, Bobby Thigpen, Alex Fernandez, Wilson Álvarez, Tim Raines, Bo Jackson, Roberto Hernández, George Bell, Charlie Hough, Ellis Burks, Jason Bere, Julio Franco, Harold Baines, Tony Phillips, Mike Cameron, Ray Durham, Albert Belle, Magglio Ordóñez, Carlos Lee, José Valentín, Joe Crede, Sandy Alomar, Aaron Rowand, Mark Buehrle, Paul Konerko, Kenny Lofton, Carl Everett, Freddy García, Roberto Alomar, Bartolo Colon, Ozzie Guillén.

This is just a sampling of the talent that played for the White Sox. Yet in this 14-year period, the team won only two post-season games and could not end a decades-long streak of not winning a World Series.

From 2000 through 2004, the White Sox hit 1,109 home runs. They plated over 4,200 runs in this short period. In 2004, they hit a franchise record 242 homers in a season and still ended up nine games out of first place during a season where they had multiple losing streaks. Despite this offensive barrage, the 2000 division title was the only post-season appearance during these years, and that ended in a huge disappointment.

By 2004, Ozzie Guillén was the manager of the White Sox. In an interview with Graham Bensinger on YouTube, Guillén stated that he was drunk when GM Kenny Williams interviewed him for the managerial job. He did have the presence of mind to ask if the interview was "for real" and he was being seriously considered for the job.

Section Two—Making History

After being told that he had the job in a second meeting, Guillén said he "went numb." Managing the White Sox had been a dream for him, he said, even though he also stated that he didn't care if he got the job or not because he was happy as a coach for the Florida Marlins.

In his first year as Sox manager, his White Sox team won 83 games. That was good for second place, but the Sox finished nine games behind the Twins.

In the 2004–2005 off-season, the Sox front office decided to change the face of the team. These changes were significant as the organization concluded that the club needed more than offense to be a serious contender.

On December 9, 2004, the White Sox announced two free agent signings. One was Jermaine Dye. Although the Sox would shift away from power somewhat, the signing of Dye would compensate for that. Dye had had three 100-RBI seasons, was usually good for home run totals in the mid–20s, and hit 33 in 2000. Dye had always been highly touted even as a rookie with Atlanta in 1996.

The other signing was Dustin Hermanson. Hermanson had had some good years as a starter but was used as a starter and reliever for the Giants in 2004. He picked up 17 saves in 2004 and would be in the Sox bullpen in 2005.

But a trade that happened four days later sent a real signal that the White Sox wanted to change the face of the team.

Carlos Lee, who had two consecutive years hitting 31 homers, was sent to the Brewers for Scott Podsednik. Podsednik saw his batting average drop 70 points in 2004, but he still picked up 70 stolen bases. The Sox clearly thought that it was beneficial to put pressure on opposition defenses by utilizing speed over power.

Then came an obscure move that didn't gain any attention at the time. On December 17, Bobby Jenks was claimed on waivers from the Anaheim Angels. Jenks was a hard-throwing right hander who had not yet pitched in the major leagues. His first appearance would be on July 6 in a mop-up role in a 7–2 win over Tampa. He pitched the ninth inning and picked up two strikeouts.

To start the new year, the Sox picked up free agent Orlando "El Duque" Hernández. Hernández had spent six seasons with the

Yankees, and his best year was in 1999, when he won 17. He would come up big in the 2005 post-season.

Three days later, the Sox made one of their most significant off-season moves. A.J. Pierzynski had spent 2004 in San Francisco after being traded there by the Twins, but now he was a member of the White Sox. Just the mention of his name says it all. He was described by some in San Francisco as a "clubhouse cancer." During a White Sox-fan luncheon in September 2023, Pierzynski said he liked playing everywhere during his career except San Francisco.

On January 27, Kenny Williams made a somewhat strange move. Although he had never seen this Japanese player in action in person, Williams signed second baseman Tadahito Iguchi. All of Iguchi's experience had been in Japan. In essence, Iguchi was a 30-year-old rookie with his almost 10-year career in Japan.

In a short period, the White Sox had picked up a new left fielder, a new right fielder, a new catcher, and a new second baseman, and added three pitchers to the staff. Every one of these players would play a significant role in the 2005 season.

In essence, the rebuilding that began with the White Flag Trade in 1997 was over. None of the six players acquired in that trade were with the club any longer, along with many key players who were on the 2000 division winners. It was time to see what a new team could do.

12

♦ ♦ ♦

Exceeding Expectations

The consensus among baseball observers was that there was nothing special about the revamped 2005 Chicago White Sox. Most expected the new-look team to finish in third. In other words, no better than when they had a team that hit the hell out of the ball.

According to Mark Gonzales, who covered the White Sox in 2005 for the *Tribune,* only two sportswriters predicted a division title for the White Sox: Larry Stone of the *Seattle Times* and Bruce Jenkins of the *San Francisco Chronicle.*[1]

In an April 3 column, Al Yellon of bleedcubbieblue.com, agreed with the consensus that the White Sox were a third-place club. In a small graph, Yellon described the 2005 White Sox this way:

HITTING: Inappropriate
PITCHING: Foreign
DEFENSE: Lousy
INTANGIBLE: Ozzie-Ball!

As for Yellon's team, the Chicago Cubs? A World Series Championship. Yellon wrote: "World Series. Yes, I'm going to do it. It was the Red Sox turn last year, now it's ours, 2005. The Cubs to win it all in a memorable seven-game series." (The seven-game series would be against the Red Sox.) Naturally, the White Sox were nowhere in Yellon's picture, since he didn't even have the team winning a wild card. In the end, he had the wrong history and the wrong team beating the Red Sox. As for the Cubs, the North Siders played sub-.500 ball in 2005 and ended up 21 games out of first place.[2]

Years later, Ozzie Guillén recalled how the Sox were overlooked

12. Exceeding Expectations

and underestimated. "I remember in spring training people were second guessing Kenny [Williams] because we got a shortstop that doesn't play every day, we got a Japanese player that never played here before, we got A.J. and everybody hates him," Guillén said in 2015.[3]

What was Ozzie-Ball, the type of ball that Al Yellon was ridiculing? It would eventually be referred to as "small ball" and would emphasize base stealing to pressure opposition defenses and moving runners along even if it meant forgoing the long ball, in an attempt to create big innings. This was illustrated by the first game of the season, which was also the home opener for the Sox.

Mark Buehrle was in a pitchers duel with Cleveland's Jake Westbrook. In the bottom of the seventh inning, the game was still scoreless. Paul Konerko led off the inning with a double. Jermaine Dye, not worrying about padding his power numbers, concentrated on moving Konerko to third. He did so with a fly to right field. Konerko scored when Indians shortstop Jhonny Peralta muffed a slow roller hit by Aaron Rowand. That would be the only run of the game in a White Sox win that took just 1:51. It was the type of game the Sox won many of in 2005.

The 1967 White Sox, who nearly won a pennant in one of the last years of pre-divisional baseball, played small ball as well. That team had to because it didn't have any power. Manager Eddie Stanky played small ball in a different way, at least with one of his starting pitchers.

According to right-hander Joe Horlen, Stanky instructed him not to worry about strikeouts. He wanted Horlen to keep the ball down to induce ground balls. Stanky told him he would buy Horlen a suit every time he could get 15 ground balls in a game, even if some resulted in hits. Horlen said he got five suits.

In 1967, the White Sox got off to a 25–15 start, and Horlen won his first eight decisions on his way to a 19-win season. Although Stanky was known as a tough, drill sergeant type of manager, Horlen had warm memories of him. "He was the only manager who fined me, and I still loved him," Horlen said to me in 1999.

In 2005, the White Sox had another right hander get off to an 8–0 start. His name was Jon Garland. Garland told me at the 2015

Section Two—Making History

SoxFest that one reason he came into his own in 2005 was because of the faith that manager Ozzie Guillén had in him. Garland recalled pitching in a tight game and Guillén came out to the mound for a conference. Garland thought he was being taken out, and he almost wanted to come out. But Guillén told the right-hander he was staying in and that he would learn to pitch in tough situations. Guillén's message was also that Garland had the *ability* to pitch in these tough situations.

At the 40-game mark in 2005, the White Sox had a 28–12 record, even better than the 1967 Sox. Garland won that 40th game, pitching seven innings of two-run ball for his eighth win.

Small ball was a big part of the first inning. Scott Podsednik led off with a single and stole second. Tadahito Iguchi sacrificed Podsednik to third. Aaron Rowand doubled Podsednik home and then stole third. Konerko drove in Rowand with a groundout to second. The Sox were able to score two runs on two hits. They won, 5–2, and won the next three games as well.

The White Sox got to show off their small ball strategy when they played a Sunday night ESPN game against the Dodgers in mid-June. They trailed Los Angeles, 3–2, going into the bottom of the eighth inning. Frank Thomas led off with a walk, and Pablo Ozuna was sent in to pinch-run. Podsednik sacrificed Ozuna to second and was able to reach first on a Dodgers error. Willie Harris bunted again, sending the runners to second and third. Aaron Rowand lined a single to left, scoring both Ozuna and Podsednik, giving the Sox a 4–3 lead. This small ball team got two runs on one hit and hung on to win, 4–3. Yet there was an even more dramatic win the night before.

Since the Dodgers had been the Sox opponent in the 1959 World Series, Sox players wore 1959-type jerseys even though many people in the ballpark had no memory or even knowledge of when the Dodgers won that Series, four games to two.

The Dodgers led, 3–1, going into the ninth inning. Then the Sox took the game away from them and looked like the world champions they were destined to be. Iguchi led off with a walk and advanced to second on a groundout by Thomas. Konerko flied out, and the Sox were one out from a loss. But Carl Everett slapped a line single to

12. Exceeding Expectations

right, scoring Iguchi. Willie Harris ran for Everett and stole second, and Rowand grounded a single up the middle, scoring Harris and tying the game.

At this point, the Dodgers' body language appeared limp. They looked defeated and were just waiting for something bad to happen. For them, it did.

A.J. Pierzynski was at the plate. Rowand took off for second and had the base stolen, but Pierzynski fouled off the pitch, and Rowand had to return to first. But the aggressive move of sending Rowand demonstrated that the Sox were not satisfied with going into extra innings. The whole inning also demonstrated that the club had other base stealing threats besides Podsednik and were not afraid to use them. If some runners got caught stealing, so be it. Regardless, Pierzynski ended the game. He took an outside pitch and went the opposite way. Dodgers outfielders J.D. Drew and Jayson Werth met at the wall in left-center. They watched helplessly as the ball landed about four rows up. The Dodgers were defeated, 5–3.

The crowd of 36,067 went wild. What was called U.S. Cellular Field was different from the old Comiskey Park in that it didn't have upper decks in the outfield. In Comiskey, the noise would get trapped inside and echo. But that night the cheering was about as loud as I ever heard it in the second park. The good crowd showed the fans believed in their team, and some may have believed it was their year.

A photo of the home plate celebration greeting Pierzynski dominated the front page of the *Tribune* sports section the next morning. The excitement of the moment was aptly captured. The Sox had won a game that seemed to be lost, maybe should have been lost.

The White Sox swept the three-game weekend series but didn't get more than six hits in any of the games. They took advantage of the few scoring opportunities they had as they began an eight-game winning streak. At the end of the streak, the Sox were 50–22, 10½ games ahead of the Twins, the team many had picked to win the division. The Sox also had the best record in the major leagues.

By the All-Star break, the Sox were still nine games ahead of the Twins. At the time, whatever league won the All-Star Game would get home field advantage in the World Series. Mark Buehrle started

Section Two—Making History

Reunion—Mark Buehrle wears the uniform of the 1959 pennant-winning White Sox. The date was June 18, 2005, as the Sox played the Dodgers, the 1959 World Series opponent. The White Sox won this game with a four-run rally in the ninth inning, demonstrating they were a legitimate contender for the post-season.

the game, gave up three hits in two scoreless innings, and picked up the win as the American League escaped a late rally and beat the National League, 7–5. If the Sox went to the World Series, they would

12. Exceeding Expectations

have the advantage of four home games, if needed. Could they make it that far? Should they have been thinking that way considering that many baseball experts expected nothing from them?

By the end of play on August 1, everything looked so good for the White Sox. They had a four-game winning streak after beating Baltimore, 6–3. A close game had been broken open by a three-run eighth inning. Buehrle picked up his 12th win, and Pierzynski hit his 16th home run. Most importantly, the Sox had a huge 15-game lead over second-place Cleveland. Everything was going so well. Clinching the AL Central seemed to be just a matter of time.

But even excellent teams have losing streaks, and the Sox had theirs in mid–August. They lost seven games in a row in different ways. However, during the last three games, the Sox managed only two runs as the offense just wasn't there.

On August 21, they faced Randy Johnson and the Yankees in Chicago. New York led, 1–0, after three innings, but the Sox had had just one hit, and it appeared the offense was still slumping. Then came the bottom of the fourth.

With one out, Iguchi tied the game with an opposite field homer into the Yankees' bullpen. Rowand followed with an opposite field home run of his own. Then Konerko hit another homer, this one going way up into the seats in straightaway left. Back-to-back-to-back home runs off Randy Johnson could not have been expected on that day or any other day.

The Sox were not done. Catcher Chris Widger hit a three-run homer to right to cap a six-run inning. The Sox didn't score again, but they wouldn't need to. Their losing streak ended with a 6–2 win, and they were still 8½ games ahead of Cleveland.

Everything seemed to right itself during early September. The White Sox went on a seven-game winning streak although they picked up only one game on the Indians. However, with a record of 87–51, everything seemed to be in hand. One more time, a division championship seemed to be just a matter of time.

Appearances can be deceiving, because times worsened. The Sox slumped again as they lost six of their next seven games. After dropping two out of three to Kansas City, manager Guillén exploded.

Section Two—Making History

"Baserunning, bad pitching," Guillén said. "If I named what I'm disappointed about we would be here all week. Even the game we won, I was disappointed. We came here and played real ugly baseball. We flat out-stink."[4]

Strong words for a first-place team that was 31 wins over .500. Yet the words "We Stink" dominated the *Tribune* sports section on the front page. Big black letters over the smaller headlines of two game stories. It ranked right up there with "we don't owe the fans anything."

Guillén said it seemed as if Cleveland was winning every day, and he, Guillén, was throwing up in the locker room every day.[5] By the time the Indians came to Chicago to play a midweek, three-game series beginning on September 19, Cleveland was only 3½ games back.

Cleveland won game one, 7–5. The White Sox led, 5–4, going into the eighth inning, but the Indians scored two runs in that inning and one more in the ninth. But almost worse than losing a slim lead in the late innings was the imagery in the bottom of the ninth.

Paul Konerko was at the plate with two men on. He represented the winning run, and wouldn't it have been great if he had homered to win the game? Instead, he popped out to second baseman Ramón Vázquez. On the follow-through of his swing, Konerko ended up down to one knee. Yes, the team's leading home run hitter went down to his knee as their closest pursuer joyfully pranced off the field. The image was haunting and was depicted on the front page of the *Tribune* sports section the next day. Konerko was shown with hands on head in frustration as he left the batter's box to run out his popup. Just a few months earlier, there had been a photo of the celebration of A.J. Pierzynski's game-winning homer against the Dodgers. Now this contrast.

"What has gotten into Joe Crede?" I heard a fan say at the ballpark one evening. Crede had been an excellent fielding third baseman since he broke into the game in September 2000. His hitting, however, was a liability. Even TV play-by-play announcer Ken Harrelson would chuckle at Crede's rusty gate type of swings. But in late 2005, something had gotten into Joe Crede.

12. Exceeding Expectations

Game two with the Indians. Tenth inning. Momentum had seemed to move Cleveland's way as they had tied things in the ninth. Joe Crede was leading off and already had hit a homer in the third inning. Using a beautiful-looking swing, Crede launched another one. From his slow exit from the batter's box, Crede thought he had another home run. And he was right. His high-arching drive to left field went flying way up into the seats. The Sox had a 7–6 win because something had gotten into Joe Crede.

Sox radio play-by-play man Ed Farmer told fans to "get off the ledge." Was he right? Was it time for fans to forget history and relax? No, it wasn't.

Cleveland won game three, 8–0. The game was competitive until the eighth inning, when the Indians scored three runs, adding three more runs in the ninth. Ex-Sox player Bobby Howry got the last five outs of the game without giving up a hit. The White Sox got but five hits in the game, all singles. Cleveland left town only 2½ games back. Minnesota was next for a four-game weekend series in Chicago.

In game one, the Sox offense went limp again. Joe Crede hit another home run, but the rest of the lineup did nothing. The Twins won, 4–1, in 11 innings. During the last 20 innings, the Sox had picked up only one run on 12 hits. It brought back memories of the banjo-hitting 1967 White Sox, who couldn't muster any offense in the waning days of the campaign.

And Cleveland? They won again, this time pounding out 15 hits and beating the Royals in Kansas City, 11–6. The Indians had now crawled to within 1½ games.

The word "choke" was now being used as the Sox had lost 13½ games in the standings in little more than six weeks. This looked worse than the 1969 Cubs, although Rick Morrissey wrote that they wouldn't be loved as the 1969 Cubs had been. He wrote that choke was an ugly word, but he still used it. "The Sox aren't choking," Morrissey wrote. "They're trying to extricate themselves from the middle of a monumental collapse brought on by a relative lack of talent. There's a difference."[6]

Ozzie Guillén got defensive. "How can you be a choker or a loser when winning 91 games?"[7] he wondered. He had a point.

Section Two—Making History

Two things happened that helped seal the division: White Sox pitching and a huge break that will be always remembered by Sox fans of that generation.

In the first inning of game two against the Twins, Jermaine Dye got the Sox started with a three-run homer. It was his 30th of the season, and the first time he hit 30 in a season since 2000. The Sox offense went limp again as they didn't score for the remainder of the game. But they didn't need the runs. José Contreras won his 14th game by throwing a complete-game six-hitter, and the Sox won, 3–1. The only downside to the evening was that Cleveland also won.

The next evening, things looked up. Dye homered again, this one an opposite field drive with two men on, in a six-run third inning. Twins manager Ron Gardenhire came out to take out his starter, Joe Mays. Mays had haunted the Sox in the past, but he didn't have it that night, going just two-plus innings. As the home run fireworks ended, the music played, and a girl about 10 years old danced in the aisle right by me. Then Joe Crede hit another home run. Everyone was happy.

Right-hander Freddy García went eight innings, and the Sox won 8–1. But so did Cleveland. Once more, the Indians had pounded lumps on the Royals. In the first three games of that series, Cleveland scored 29 runs. They had won 17 out of their last 19 games. Yes, it seemed like they were winning every day. The lead for the Sox was still at 1½ games.

Then came the September 25 game.

First, Mark Buehrle pitched a brilliant, four-hit complete game to beat the Twins, 4–1, to win the series. The Sox offense was limited to five hits, but one was a two-run homer by Paul Konerko, his 38th. In the final three games, the Sox bullpen threw but one inning. Even in the first-game loss, starter Brandon McCarthy went eight innings and gave up only one run. The solid starting pitching was a sign of things to come in a historic post-season.

Now for the break the Sox had been waiting for, and it seemed like this was the only way Cleveland could lose. The Indians and the Royals were tied in the bottom of the ninth inning. Kansas City had a runner, Ángel Berroa, on second base with one out. Catcher Paul Phillips hit

12. Exceeding Expectations

what looked like a routine fly to center. Grady Sizemore was in position to make the catch. But he lost it in the bright Sunday sun, and it dropped to the dark green Kaufmann Stadium outfield grass. Berroa scored for the Royals, and the Indians finally lost a game, 5–4. (Sizemore would go on to win Gold Gloves in 2007 and 2008.)

The loss seemed to take the steam out of the Indians. They had been playing at such a torrid pace, they had to hit a bad stretch sometime. They were still only 2½ games behind and caught a break in the schedule. Tampa Bay, last in the AL East, was coming into Cleveland next for a three-game series.

But the poor Indians lost the first two games of the series with one-run losses. They lost the second game, 1–0, as their once-hot offense had wilted. Cleveland posted a 6–0 win in the last game, but time had run out. They had posted 18–9 records in August and September, but it hadn't been enough.

In Detroit on September 28, the Tigers' Placido Polanco faced reliever Bobby Jenks in the bottom of the ninth inning, representing the tying run with two outs. Polanco lined out to Konerko to secure the White Sox a 4–2 win. Konerko hit his 40th homer in the game, the second consecutive season he had reached the 40-homer plateau.

The White Sox had clinched the AL Central. For all the consternation, angst, and throwing up, the Sox had been in first place from the first day of the season. No curses, no repetition of history, no mind-boggling collapses.

There had been the talk that maybe the Sox just weren't good enough and that the Indians were the better team. Shouldn't they have done more at the trading deadline? They had picked up Geoff Blum, but that was it? Despite these outside distractions and the dredging up of history, the White Sox had held on and won. It was their first division title in five years, and the toughest one to win as the Indians and bad memories had been bearing down on them.

Of course, there were the champagne showers. Relieved fans could feel the wetness of their hair, the stinging in their eyes. For fans, there were probably tears of relief. There was no Chicago-type baseball collapse after all.

But now it was time to see if real history could be made.

13

◆ ◆ ◆

The American League in the Post-Season

4–3, 9–3, 11–1, 3–0, 7–3, 3–1, 6–3, 7–4, 5–2.

These are the scores of White Sox post-season losses at home since 1959. It was a dubious nine-game losing streak. Between 1920 and 2004, they had won only one post-season game at home. That was the 11–0 win over the Dodgers in the first game of the 1959 World Series. Ted Kluszewski, a slugging first baseman who had biceps so big that he wore sleeveless jerseys, hit two homers. Thirty-nine-year-old Early Wynn, a man nasty enough to brush back his own mother, pitched seven scoreless innings. That was it for winning a post-season game at home for the next 45 years. The 1959 team may have been lost in an historical vacuum, but many fans in 2005 knew of or had experienced the home game post-season losing streak. Or at least some of it.

The first hurdle for the White Sox in the 2005 playoffs was the defending 2004 champion Boston Red Sox. Their World Series win the year before had ended a long drought of their own. Ironically, their last championship came in 1918, when they beat the Cubs. But according to author Sean Deveney in his book, *The Original Curse,* 1919 was not the first Series to be fixed. He claimed that some of the 1919 White Sox players had heard that the Cubs had thrown the 1918 Series and got away with it. The Black Sox scandal followed. "If we really look at the lives of the ball players in 1918," Deveney wrote, "if we really picture what it was like to walk a mile in their caps, then we can see that a fix not only a possibility but is understandable and excusable."[1]

13. The American League in the Post-Season

Deveney theorized that with the combination of World War I and a bad United States economy, it was possible that there would be no major league baseball in 1919, and players needed to make some money before things collapsed. He also stated that players felt little loyalty to their teams because they felt they were getting cheated regarding World Series shares.

Of course, this is conjecture based partly on circumstantial evidence, even though Sox fans would feel better to believe the Cubs threw a World Series first. But the reality in 2005 was that the White Sox first had to face a tough Red Sox team that had won 95 games and had post-season success which included coming back from a three-games-to-zero deficit to defeat their arch-rival Yankees in the ALCS. They had David Ortiz and Manny Ramirez, who combined for 92 home runs and 292 RBI during the regular season.

In Game 1, José Contreras was on the hill for the White Sox, facing 13-game winner Matt Clement of the Red Sox. In the first inning, Contreras got into a jam when he gave up a one-out double to Edgar Renteria. But he struck out Ortiz and got Ramirez to ground out to third to complete a clean inning.

Then came the White Sox first, which set the tone for the rest of the game. Podsednik started things off, and he got nicked by a Clement pitch. Iguchi sacrificed Podsednik to second with a well-executed bunt that dribbled about 10 feet from home plate. Dye was also hit by a pitch.

Konerko was next, and during his at-bat, Podsednik stole third. Konerko hit a ground ball behind third base. Bill Mueller threw to second to force Dye, and Podsednik scored. It was typical 2005 White Sox baseball. They had picked up a run without getting a hit or even hitting the ball out of the infield. (Konerko had almost homered, but his long drive to left excited the crowd until the fans realized the ball had curved around the foul pole.)

Carl Everett singled hard to right for the White Sox's first hit. Aaron Rowand followed with a flare that dropped into left-center to drive in Konerko.

Then came the big hit of the inning. Pierzynski homered. His opposite field hit landed in almost the same spot as when he hit the game-winning homer against the Dodgers back in June. The White Sox, who had scored about 100 fewer runs than the Red Sox during the season, had opened the game with a five-run inning. As Pierzynski rounded the bases, a fan held up a sign that read: "2004—Their Sox. 2005—Our Sox."

In the White Sox third, Konerko would not be deprived of a homer. His drive to straightaway left field landed deep in the bullpen, and the White Sox led, 6–0.

In the top of the fourth inning, the Red Sox were able to score two runs partly because of uncharacteristically sloppy play by the White Sox. Trot Nixon started things with a single. Jason Varitek, seeing that third baseman Joe Crede was playing back, laid down a nice bunt down the line. Crede tried to barehand the ball and ended up knocking it all the way back to home plate. Nixon ended up on third base, and Varitek made it all the way to second on a ball that travelled only about 40 feet.

Contreras then threw a truly wild pitch that was way outside and in the dirt. Nixon scored easily, and Varitek walked to third. Kevin Millar doubled to right to drive in Varitek. Dye dove in an attempt to make the catch but didn't come close, and the ball rolled to the wall. The White Sox crowd went silent as Contreras had already given up seven hits, and it appeared the powerful Red Sox were ready to rally.

Guillén went out to talk to Contreras. Guillén would tell ESPN announcers after the game that he told Contreras to concentrate on the hitters and not worry about who was on base. To the relief of White Sox fans, Contreras got out of the inning with no further damage. In fact, the Red Sox would not score again in the game.

The White Sox answered immediately in the bottom of the inning. Pierzynski got another hit when he doubled down the right field line. One out later, Juan Uribe got into the act when he picked on a hanging breaking pitch and homered deep into the left field seats. Clement was done for the day, and the rout was on.

In the sixth inning, the White Sox scored four runs, three coming on a home run by Podsednik, who ripped a low-inside pitch down the right field line and well over the wall. He had not homered during the regular season. (Later in the post-season, Podsednik would hit an even more dramatic home run.)

Pierzynski led off the eighth inning with his second homer of the game. This one he pulled to right field. For the day, the White Sox catcher had two homers, a double, four runs driven in, and four runs scored. It was one of the best days a White Sox player ever experienced in the post season.

Despite the lopsided score, there was still some excitement in the ninth inning. John Olerud, in a pinch-hitting role, sent a deep fly to left-center. Aaron Rowand, even with his team far ahead, went crashing into the wall in pursuit. He got his glove on the ball but was unable to hold onto it, and Olerud picked up a double. Rowand got up looking a little dazed but stayed in the game. This was the way he played center field. (In the late 1960s, the White Sox had another center fielder who played the same way. In old Comiskey, the center field fence was only about five feet high. Once, when center fielder Ken Berry was chasing a ball hit by the Twins' Tony Oliva, Berry threw his whole body over the fence in an attempt to make the catch. He climbed back onto the field without the ball.)

Tony Graffanino ended the game when he sent Podsednik all the way to the left field wall. Podsednik reached above the top of the wall to make the homer-saving catch.

Final score: White Sox 14, Red Sox 2. It was quite a way to end that post-season losing streak at home that had stretched out over 46 years. It was total domination in almost every facet of the game. But this didn't mean the Series was going to get easy. The White Sox were still facing the defending world champions.

Break Number One

Good teams get fortunate at times. In fact, good luck will occur many times when two talented and well-matched teams play each other. Somebody makes a mistake they normally don't make, and it turns out to be costly. Some fans who remember the 1983 American League playoffs haven't forgiven Jerry Dybzinski for his baserunning gaffe, even it almost made sense that something like that would allow

Section Two—Making History

one team to win. The White Sox were the beneficiaries of some good fortune in the 2005 post-season, and the first such fortune occurred in the second game of the Division Series against Boston.

Mark Buehrle was on the mound for the White Sox and was not his usual sharp self. He gave up two runs in both the first and third innings. Meanwhile, Red Sox starter David Wells cruised through the first four innings, giving up only two hits. By the bottom of the fifth, the score stood at 4–0, Red Sox.

The White Sox mounted a little comeback. Carl Everett started things off with an opposite field single. Aaron Rowand followed with a double down the left field line that hit the base line chalk. Everett scored. A. J. Pierzynski was next and gave himself up by grounding out to second to advance Rowand to third. Pierzynski applauded himself as he returned to the dugout, happy he had done the small ball thing. Joe Crede hit a grounder up the middle to score Rowand. The score now stood at 4–2, and White Sox fans began singing "We will rock you."

Juan Uribe hit a slow-rolling grounder to second baseman Tony Graffanino that had the possibility of being an inning-ending double play. But before attempting to start the double play, Graffanino let the ball slip though his legs. Crede moved to third, and Uribe took his place at first.

How could this have happened with a sure fielder like Graffanino? Since the ball was hit slowly, Graffanino could have been in a hurry to get the first out at second. He should have gotten the sure out by taking his time, but catastrophe hit him first. The ball trickled into short right field. (Catastrophe also struck ESPN announcer and Red Sox lover Chris Berman. "Oh no!" Berman screamed, "everyone is safe!" Yes, Chris, everyone was safe. You could pick up your objectivity again once the game is over.)

For a moment, it appeared the error would not be too costly. Scott Podsednik fouled out to third baseman Bill Mueller. Wells had seemed to find himself again, and now he only needed to get past Tadahito Iguchi to escape the inning still two runs ahead.

Wells threw a beautiful breaking pitch that had Iguchi fooled. It worked so well, Wells decided to throw another one. Big mistake.

13. The American League in the Post-Season

Iguchi lined the second breaking pitch into the left field seats for a three-run homer. Suddenly the White Sox led, 5–4.

Chris Berman found his objectivity a little earlier than thought. He said, "you cannot afford to give a good team like the White Sox extra outs." Berman was right. The White Sox got a break and took big advantage of it. Meanwhile, Buehrle gave Iguchi a grateful hug in the dugout. Judging from his huge smile, Iguchi enjoyed the affection.

Break Number Two—a Rough Final Two Innings

A frustrated Rich Gossage told me sometime before the 2005 post-season that he wasn't all that impressed with closers who only pitch the ninth inning. He said he often came in during the eighth inning, and sometimes even in the seventh. What was the big deal? (The hard-throwing Gossage did receive recognition for his career when he was elected the Hall of Fame in 2008. He basically had one pitching philosophy: A batter can't hit what he can't see.)

In Game 2 against Boston, White Sox manager Ozzie Guillén decided to bring in his big closer in the eighth inning with the score still 5–4. It was none other than Bobby Jenks, the young man who had played in his first major league game back in July.

The first hitter Jenks faced was Manny Ramirez. Ramirez whacked a low fastball on a line to center, but it was right at Aaron Rowand. If Ramirez had gotten some lift under that ball, he would have tied the game with a home run. Instead, it was just a scary out. Jason Varitek followed with a conventional out when he tapped a hopper right to Jenks. Now Jenks only needed four outs to pick up his Gossage-like save.

Left-handed Trot Nixon was the potential third out of the inning. He launched a high and deep drive down the right field line. It had more than enough distance for a game-tying homer, but unfortunately for Nixon it was foul by a wide margin. Jenks decided to pitch him away and ended up walking him.

Bill Mueller was up next, and he hit a shot on the ground. But it was right at Iguchi and became the third out. Jenks had to let out a breath as he walked to the dugout. Three hard-hit balls, and the Red Sox couldn't get a man past first base.

The White Sox failed to score in their half of the eighth inning, and Jenks returned to the mound again to protect a one-run lead.

Things started out well when John Olerud tapped out to Jenks. Tony Graffanino was next, hoping to atone for his error. And he did. He lined a shot into the left-center field gap. Podsednik made a diving stop, but the hustling Graffanino slid safely into second, putting himself in scoring position. Podsednik still made a good play, though. That hit could have gotten past him, and Graffanino could have ended up at third with only one out. Still, the Red Sox had some life.

Johnny Damon followed and worked the count full. Jenks threw a high-inside fastball that had some late movement. A jammed Damon fouled out to Pierzynski. Edgar Renteria, who had two hits, was the last chance for the Red Sox. He hit a two-hopper to Juan Uribe at shortstop, and the game was over. Jenks had to work hard and sweated some, but he had a save that would have made Rich Gossage proud.

At a televised post-game press conference, in reference to the Graffanino error, Ozzie Guillén said, "Sometimes you get lucky." Yes, Ozzie, sometimes you get lucky.

The Curse in Reverse

It was almost as if the pressure was on the White Sox as they headed to Boston for Game 3. While Chicago had won the first two games, there was the knowledge that the Red Sox had come back from that 3–0 lead the Yankees had the year before. It helped the Red Sox earn their first World Series championship since 1918. As with the Cubs, the Red Sox fans felt their team was cursed. Boston had lost the seventh and deciding game in the World Series in 1967, 1975, and 1986. Nineteen eighty-six was the most heartbreaking defeat as the Red Sox needed one more out to clinch in the sixth game. They couldn't get that out and ended up losing partly because of the famous Bill Buckner error. The former Cub, Bill Buckner. But

13. The American League in the Post-Season

there isn't such a thing as a curse even though Buckner wore a Cubs batting glove under his fielding glove.

In Game 3 against Boston, in the top of the third inning with the game scoreless and two out, the White Sox, in a way, played small ball again. Tim Wakefield was on the mound for Boston and had gotten the first eight White Sox hitters out, with a solid defense behind him. Finally, Juan Uribe picked up the first Chicago hit with a double high off the Green Monster (the 37 foot-two-inch high left field wall at Fenway Park).

Podsednik doubled by going the opposite way. Uribe scored as Podsednik's drive rolled to the corner. Iguchi grounded a single to center that drove in Podsednik. Dye dropped a single to right for the fourth straight hit. Konerko ended the inning with a fly ball, but he had stroked it to right as he went with the pitch. Some hitters don't like playing in Fenway because the Green Monster is so close and inviting. But only the free-swinging Uribe pulled the ball. The White Sox just missed having a big inning as a result.

The White Sox's 2–0 advantage vanished in the fourth inning. David Ortiz and Manny Ramirez began the inning with back-to-back solo homers. For a moment, in the bottom of the fifth, it appeared that the Red Sox were ready to take a three-run lead. With two out, Johnny Damon hit a soft flare down the right field line for a double. Edgar Renteria walked, and home run threat David Ortiz came to the plate.

Ortiz took a healthy cut at a Freddy García breaking pitch. Ortiz stood at the plate looking like he thought he got all of it. But the ball sailed to the deepest part of the ballpark, and Aaron Rowand caught it standing in the middle of the warning track. It's 420 to dead center in Fenway, and the drive could have been a home run in other parks or at least a tougher catch for an outfielder. In this case, Rowand had time to camp under the ball and make a routine catch.

The White Sox picked up two more runs in the top of the sixth inning when Konerko hit a two-run homer high over the Green Monster and out of the park. The pitch had gotten in on Konerko somewhat, but he was still able to extend his arms. It was just another key hit in the post-season for Konerko, and it chased Wakefield from the game.

Section Two—Making History

Then came the bottom of the sixth inning, another remarkable inning the White Sox would play in their history-making postseason.

The inning opened with another home run by Manny Ramirez. Left-handed Damaso Marte came in for García and loaded the bases by giving up a single to Trot Nixon and walks to Bill Mueller and John Olerud. It looked like Boston was taking control of the game. Ozzie Guillén summoned Orlando "El Duque" Hernández from the pen. The inning became one of the most memorable in White Sox history.

Jason Varitek was first to face Hernández. He swung at a 2–1 pitch that was a little up in the zone, if it was indeed in the zone. The result was a foul pop that Konerko caught near the on-deck circle as he charged in from first base.

Tony Graffanino followed as the crowd chanted, "Tony, Tony." Graffinino battled Hernández for 10 pitches, including three full-count fouls. Before the last pitch, Pierzynski made a mound visit to make sure he and his pitcher were communicating. Hernandez threw a nice-looking, off-speed breaking pitch that sank down to knee level. Graffanino was ahead of the pitch, and he sent a weak pop-up to Uribe, who had come in a few feet at shortstop. The bases were still loaded, but now with two down.

Johnny Damon, who had 197 hits during the regular season, was up. He, too, battled Hernández to a full count. Again, Pierzynski made a mound visit. Hernández again threw an off-speed offering. This pitch was low, and Damon tried to stop his swing. Red Sox fans cheered because they thought Damon had walked to force in the game-tying run. But home plate umpire Mark Wegner signaled that Damon had gone too far, calling him out on strikes. Hernández ran into the dugout, thrilled he had gotten out of a bases-loaded jam with no damage. The White Sox still led by one run.

(Note: There was a sidebar to this inning. It appeared that Pierzynski trapped the last pitch. Damon hadn't noticed and made no attempt to run out a dropped third strike. Taking no chances, Pierzynski tagged Damon before tossing the ball back to the mound. This type of thinking would prove valuable in another game.)

13. The American League in the Post-Season

El Duque—Orlando "El Duque" Hernández confers with catcher A.J. Pierzynski during the bases-loaded, no-out jam against Boston in the third game of the ALDS. Hernández got out of the jam in dramatic fashion, getting two infield popups and a strikeout of Johnny Damon. It was just another dramatic inning in the 2005 post-season.

In the top of the ninth inning, the White Sox played small ball again. Pierzynski led off with a double off the Green Monster in left-center. Joe Crede bunted him to third. Juan Uribe also bunted, this time a safety squeeze. Red Sox pitcher Mike Timlin tried to nail Pierzynski at the plate, but his throw was too late. The White Sox had an insurance run.

Some ridiculed the "small ball" concept, pointing out that the White Sox hit 200 home runs during the regular season, the sixth consecutive time they pulled off that feat. Yet the White Sox had been playing for one run all season long. It was Ozzie Guillén's philosophy, and his players bought into it. In addition, although many major leaguers are not good bunters, but the White Sox were successful at moving runners along this way. Their record in one-run games in 2005 was 35–19, which was key in getting the team to the post-season. They executed in many ways, and it allowed them to win close, low-scoring games. Of course, an occasional walk-off home run helped, too.

Hernández threw three scoreless innings, and Bobby Jenks came in to close the game in the ninth. The ball never left the infield in a three-up, three-down inning. Edgar Renteria made the last out with a groundout to Tadahito Iguchi. The Boston Red Sox were world champions no more. Chris Berman described his Red Sox as "valiant," but the valiant Red Sox had been swept.

As for the Chicago White Sox, it was their first post-season series win since 1917, when the unfortunate Shoeless Joe Jackson was on the team. The 1917 squad beat the New York Giants, four games to two, in the World Series. By the time the White Sox beat the Red Sox in 2005, the Giants had been in San Francisco for almost 50 years.

It was a huge moment for the White Sox. Since divisional play began in 1969, their post-season record was 3–10. They had gotten that big break with the Graffanino error in Game 2, but they had played the game Ozzie Guillén's way and had outplayed Boston.

Now it was onto the ALCS.

14

◆ ◆ ◆

One Last Stop to the World Series

From 1951 through 1967, the Chicago White Sox had their most successful run in franchise history. The team put together 17 straight winning seasons, including three consecutive 90-plus-win seasons from 1963 through 1965. Yet even as they put up those impressive win totals, they couldn't get past the New York Yankees. During this period, the Yankees won an amazing 12 pennants. The 1959 campaign was the only time the White Sox went to the World Series during this era. The White Sox had some excellent players but just couldn't match up to the New York's powerful and more balanced lineups that included future Hall of Famers.

The 1964 season was the most for the White Sox. In mid–August, the Sox swept the Yankees in a four-game series at home. In the last game, Chicago beat the great Whitey Ford, 5–0, in a Thursday day game. Midweek day games usually didn't draw as well as night or weekend contests. But this game drew 36,667 fans. More importantly, the Sox sat in first place, 4½ games ahead of New York. In fact, the Yankees were in third place, four games behind second-place Baltimore. The Yankees added to their losing streak by dropping two more games to Boston.

Was this finally the year the White Sox could sneak past New York? Well, no. History repeated itself. In September, New York went on an 11-game winning streak. The White Sox won their last nine games but still ended up in second place, one game out. They had won 98 games, at that time their second-best win total in team history. But in 1964, Major League Baseball only had two 10-team leagues.

Section Two—Making History

There were no divisions and no wild card teams. Even though the White Sox had the second-best record in baseball, they went home and watched the World Series on television. The Yankees lost the Series in seven games to St. Louis, but that brought little comfort to White Sox fans.

So who went to the World Series in 2000 when the White Sox won a league-leading 95 games? The Yankees. Who won that World Series? The Yankees.

White Sox fans would have loved to see their 2005 team beat the Yankees in the post-season. Instead, the Los Angeles Angels of Anaheim had bested the Yankees in five games in their division series. The Angels would certainly provide enough competition. They had won the Series in 2002 and were coming off their second straight division title. The Angels were not to be taken lightly.

But there was a little twist to things. The Angels had played Game 4 of the Yankees series in New York, then travelled all the way back to California to advance, and now, on the third consecutive night, were playing in a different city. Angels players were shown on television walking into their hotel early in the morning before the sun rose. Whatever sleep the Angels were able to get had been on the airplane.

As for the White Sox, they had plenty of rest because they had swept Boston. In addition, they were able to set their rotation and have their hottest pitcher, José Contreras, start Game 1. It was almost unfair as the Angels had to travel from the West Coast to an opposition's ballpark under bad scheduling.

But Game 1 turned out to be a big win for the Angels. Contreras pitched a decent game, giving up three runs in 8⅓ innings. However, the White Sox scored just two runs and failed to score after the fourth inning. If the Angels could win Game 2, they'd head back home with all the pressure heaped on the White Sox.

In that pivotal Game 2, Mark Buehrle threw a complete game, giving up one lone run on five hits. Yet his performance was completely overshadowed by one of the most controversial plays in post-season history. The Angels were incensed, and the White Sox were accused of cheating. More accurately, their catcher was accused of cheating.

14. One Last Stop to the World Series

Break Number Three

The game was tied, 1–1, in the bottom of the ninth inning. Everyone's favorite person, A.J. Pierzynski was at the plate with two outs and two strikes. Kelvim Escobar threw an off-speed breaking pitch, and a lunging Pierzynski swung over the top of it. Catcher Josh Paul, thinking the inning was over, tossed the ball toward the mound. Pierzynski, thinking that Paul had trapped the pitch, ran to first on what he believed was a dropped third strike. The Angels were stunned and almost speechless. What was Pierzynski doing?

Angels manager Mike Scioscia was livid. But home plate umpire Doug Eddings backed Pierzynski, and the White Sox catcher remained on first. It was an incredible call. The irate Angels remained on the field. Pablo Ozuna ran for Pierzynski and stole second without even drawing a throw. Now, a disputed dropped third strike had helped put a runner in scoring position. The *winning run*.

Joe Crede, who recently had some dramatic late-inning hits, was up. Using his picture-perfect swing, Crede lined a shot on an 0–2 pitch off the middle of the left field wall, right down the line, missing a home run by a few feet. The homer was not needed. Ozuna cruised home, and the White Sox had evened the series with a 2–1 win. Crede did his small ball thing by taking two strikes, allowing Ozuna to steal on the second pitch. He ripped an inside offering from Kelvim Escobar to win the game. Fox TV Sports announcers Joe Buck and Tim McCarver were as livid as the Angels.

Replays were not used to check umpire calls until 2008. The Angels could not protest. But what would have happened if replay was used? Was there enough evidence to overturn Eddings' call? Probably not, but who really knows?

Many piled on Pierzynski, but there were two factors that defend his action. The first was the Johnny Damon strikeout in the Boston series with the bases loaded. Damon stood in the batter's box in frustration after being called out. He had made no move toward first base even though it appeared Pierzynski had trapped the third strike. The baserunner approaching home plate stopped and made no attempt to

Section Two—Making History

In the most controversial moment of the 2005 post-season, A.J. Pierzynski heads to first base, thinking the Angels' catcher trapped a pitch on a third strike. Josh Paul, thinking the inning is over, tosses the ball toward the mound. Pierzynski was awarded first base, and the White Sox won on a Joe Crede double. Pierzynski was accused of cheating. The irate Angels went back to California and lost three straight home games. The "dropped third strike" is considered a turning point in the ALCS.

step on the plate. Pierzynski took no chances. He stepped over and gently tagged Damon. The inning was officially over.

Secondly, Pierzynski told sports reporter Teddy Greenstein years later that he had been victimized in a similar way when he played in San Francisco. Pierzynski said the batter had even returned to the dugout before running to first. But the umpire gave the hitter the base. With this past experience, Pierzynski took off. Was he cheating? Until this day, he says no. Regardless, the play haunts his playing legacy even though he had a solid career with 2,043 hits.[1]

While the Angels had every right to be angry, Escobar had the count in his favor on Crede. Get him out, and the Pierzynski gambit means nothing. But he threw a hitter's pitch on a two-strike count that was inside but didn't jam Crede. He was able to extend his arms, and he almost sent it out of the ballpark.

14. One Last Stop to the World Series

In addition, there was no guarantee the Angels would have won in extra innings. They had scored but one run on eight hits in their last 15 innings. Just what was going on with their offense? As it would turn out, not much.

15

♦ ♦ ♦

Game Three

Anaheim

If the White Sox were accused of cheating, at least no one said they were doing it 1919-style, trying to lose to make money on the side. Regardless, the Angels were not in such bad shape. The series was tied, and they had three straight games at home. Win two of three at home, split the last two games in Chicago, and go to the World Series. That's how it is done during the regular season, isn't it? Win big at home and play .500 ball on the road.

The Angels had John Lackey on the mound for Game 3. Lackey was 14–5 with a 3.44 ERA during the 2005 season. They had to feel good about their Game 3 chances even if their offense was still having difficulties.

Scott Podsednik led the game off with a line drive single to right. Again, playing small ball, Iguchi sacrificed Podsednik to second. Dye followed with a gapper to right-center, driving in Podsednik. Dye stood on the second with a double.

Lackey was hanging his breaking pitches, and he hung one to Konerko. The Sox cleanup hitter smacked a drive that cleared the 387 mark in left center with plenty to spare. The game had barely started, and the Sox already led, 3–0.

Chicago extended their lead with an RBI single by Carl Everett in the third inning and another RBI single by Konerko in the fifth. The White Sox won, 5–2. Sounds like a boring game, and in a way, it was. The Anaheim crowd tried to get into things but never really could because their team got four measly hits. The game was over in a little over two and a half hours.

15. Game Three

For the White Sox, this was all good. Jon Garland threw a complete game. He walked the first Angels hitter, but that runner was wiped out on a double play. It was Iguchi doing an acrobatic move of sorts as he caught a high hopper by second base and whipped the ball to first. Garland did not walk a batter for the rest of the game. He gave up a two-run homer to Orlando Cabrera in the sixth inning but got the remaining 10 batters in order to put the game away. Garland showed some durability as he threw just under 120 pitches.

The 3–4–5 hitters in the Sox lineup drove in all the runs. Chicago should have scored more, but they ran into good pitching by Angels reliever Brendan Donnelly. As it turned out, they didn't need the extra runs.

In the second inning for the Angels, Darin Erstad was thrown out at third base trying to stretch a double into a triple with two outs. Erstad was out by a mile and was not even able to reach third base. Why he allowed himself to get thrown out at third for the last out of inning was a mystery. The game stood at only 3–0 in the early stages, so there was no need to try to do something big. Were the Angels allowing the dropped third strike to get to them?

This was a typical 2005 White Sox win. They got good pitching, made no errors, and otherwise didn't give any help to the opposition. They had a mixture of small ball and power. The Angels had to know they were in trouble.

16

♦ ♦ ♦

Game 4

*Almost as If It Was Fixed—
In a Different Way*

As mentioned throughout this story, the White Sox found all kinds of ways not to go to the World Series during their over 100-year history. Some of it was bad luck, some of it self-inflicted. But in Game 4 against the Angels, everything went their way, and it doomed the California team to a frustrating end. In fact, it was amazing how *everything* went the Sox's way.

In the first inning, the White Sox played their usual combination of small ball and power. Podsednik led off things with a walk against Angels starter Ervin Santana. Santana was ahead of Podsednik 0–2 but lost him. Still having trouble with his command, Santana hit Iguchi with a pitch.

Dye hit a fly to medium-deep center. Steve Finley made the catch and made the right move by throwing to second base, since Podsednik would have an easy time getting to third. But even with the throw, Iguchi took off from first base and was able to slide into second safely.

Cleanup hitter Konerko stepped in with a good RBI opportunity. The Angels infield played back, willing to concede a run. Almost anything could bring in a run, and the White Sox had the chance to open the scoring without getting a hit.

But Konerko did more than that. For the second game in a row, he homered to left field. One more time, his team had a 3–0 lead. The Angels were already in a hole with a slumping offense. However, a strange bottom of the second inning sent the Angels reeling.

16. Game 4

With one out, Darin Erstad walked. Casey Kotchman followed with a soft, high bouncer to the right of the mound. Sox starter Freddy García made an off-balance throw to first base that sailed over Konerko's head, sending Erstad to third and Kotchman to second. Bengie Molina blooped a single to center. The Angels had their first run of the game, and a chance for more with men on first and third and only one out. Disaster followed, at least for the Angels.

Break Number Four

Steve Finley hit a ground ball to second base, but clearly Pierzynski interfered with his swing as his glove hit Finley's bat. Catcher interference should have been called, but home plate umpire Ron Kulpa did nothing and let the play go on. On his way to first base, Finley looked back at Kulpa, but Kulpa still made no call. Meanwhile, the White Sox completed a double play, and the inning was over.

An interference call would have given the Angels the bases loaded with one out. García wasn't looking real sharp. The Angels would have had a great chance to put up a crooked number and perhaps make a come-from-behind effort that would have been a great momentum builder. Instead, they ended the inning with just one run.

What if Finley had just run the play out without making his plea to the umpire? He would have beaten the relay to first. The Angels would have plated another run and cut the Sox lead to one. In addition, their inning would have still been alive with a chance to score more. But those are just "would haves."

Was there really catcher interference? Of course there was. The replay definitely showed Finley's bat coming in solid contact with Pierzynski's glove. Pierzynski even put his glove behind his back, trying to hide what happened. After the game, Pierzynski didn't want to talk much about the play with a Fox TV interviewer. No one could blame him.

In the top of the third inning, the White Sox got the run right back. Dye got on base because of an uncharacteristic error by Orlando Cabrera. He eventually scored on a Carl Everett single to center. Once more, the Sox scored with the benefit of only one hit.

Section Two—Making History

There was nothing fluky about the way the White Sox scored in the top of the fourth inning. Pierzynski socked a 430-foot homer to dead center. The White Sox led, 5–1. For the Angels, more bad luck ensued in the top of the fifth. Podsednik again led off the inning with a walk. Santana attempted a pickoff. The home Anaheim crowd booed because they thought Podsednik was out on a close play. The fans were right. The replay clearly showed that Podsednik got tagged before his hand could reach the bag. But with no replay challenge in effect, the call stood.

What did Podsednik do? He stole second base and remained there until there were two outs and Konerko coming up. The Angels wanted no part of the homer-hitting Konerko, so they intentionally walked him even though that set up righty Scot Shields to face the left-handed-hitting Carl Everett. Everett picked up his second RBI with a sharply hit single to left. The inning should have ended long before. Instead, again, the White Sox scored with only one hit.

In the seventh inning, Podsednik again led off with a walk. He stole second as another call went against the Angels. The replay again showed that Podsednik was out. The Angels took some solace in the fact that Podsednik did not score in the inning.

Joe Crede picked up a two–run single in the eighth inning, and the rout was on. White Sox starter Freddy García had settled down after the rocky and potentially disastrous second inning. He threw the third straight complete game for the Chicago pitching staff, giving up six hits and walking only one. So far, four games into the Series, the Chicago relief corps had thrown just two-thirds of an inning.

The Angels had to be lamenting the second inning and the "non-call" by the home player umpire. The game could have been so different. First, the dropped third strike call, and then the non-call. They had to think that they could have been up three games to one instead of the other way around. No matter how hard they had tried to keep things in perspective, the Angels had to feel deflated.

This didn't take anything away from the White Sox effort. They scored eight runs on eight hits. Their leadoff hitter got on base four

16. Game 4

times. García made a costly error, but the defense tightened up after that. The Sox starter went the distance once more.

The Los Angeles Angels of Anaheim must have felt cursed. But, of course there is no such thing as a curse.

17

◆ ◆ ◆

Game Five
On the Verge of Making History

On October 16, 2005, the White Sox stood in an unfamiliar circumstance. Since divisional play had begun in 1969, they had never faced a situation in which, if they won a game, they would go to the World Series.

Before 2005, the Sox had won three divisional titles and no wild card berths. They lost all three post-season series and didn't take any series to a deciding game. Yet now, with a win, they would be on their way to the World Series. No Chicago baseball team had been to a Series in 46 years. The Cubs had been five outs away in 2003, but then there was Steve Bartman and their imagined curse. But as we all know, there is no such thing as a curse.

Game 5 in Anaheim had a strange atmosphere. The temperature in Anaheim was mild, but the night seemed even darker with an overcast sky and rain. It looked more like Chicago than California. Angels fans had to feel the gloom of the darkness as their team had to face José Contreras for the second time. Paul Byrd, the winner of Game 1, would go for the Angels.

The Angels were frustrated. They felt that every call had gone against them, and the Series didn't reflect what could have been. To them, the dropped third strike was a travesty, and White Sox baserunners were called safe when they were out. However, there was no getting around the fact that the Angels were doing next to nothing at the plate and otherwise were playing sloppy baseball.

The White Sox opened the scoring in the second inning in their

17. Game Five

typical 2005 way. Aaron Rowand dropped a double just inside the right field line that bounced into the stands. A.J. Pierzynski stepped up to a smattering of boos. He laid a bunt down the third base line that forced the third baseman to come in, allowing Rowand to advance easily. Joe Crede sent a fly ball to medium-deep center, and Rowand scored easily. Again, yet again, the White Sox scored with the benefit of just one hit.

In the bottom of the third inning, the White Sox played a little give-away. Juan Rivera began the inning with a double, and Angels fans tried to make some noise. Contreras tried to pick Rivera off and threw the ball into center field, sending Rivera to third. He walked home on an Adam Kennedy single.

The Angels later took their first lead since their 3–1 advantage in Game 1. That two-run margin would be their largest of the series. It was the bottom of the fifth inning when Adam Kennedy led off with an infield single. With a hit-and-run on, Shone Figgins tomahawked a Contreras offering toward the right field corner. Angels Stadium has a short wall in the right field corner. A fan in the front row reached over and got himself a souvenir when he caught the ball on the bounce. Kennedy was stopped at third base. This brought Angels manager Mike Scioscia out to protest, saying Kennedy would have scored easily if the fan hadn't interfered. The umpires agreed and sent Kennedy home to score. It was the first break of the series for the Angels even with Figgens kept at second base though he would have had a triple if the fan had kept his mitts to himself.

It turned out not to matter as Figgins scored on a sacrifice fly. The Angels, to the rare delight of their fans, led 3–2. But they would not get a baserunner for the remainder of the game.

Kelvim Escobar, the losing pitcher in Game 2, came in to pitch the top of the seventh inning. He had given up the game-winning double to Joe Crede in Game 2. Now Crede was leading off.

On a pitch similar to the one in Game 2, Crede tied the game with a home run that cleared the left field fence by a lot. That had to feel strange to Escobar, but more strangeness was on its way. Once again, it would involve A.J. Pierzynski.

Escobar settled down. In fact, he struck out the next five hitters as White Sox batters kept swinging over the top of his breaking pitches. Escobar appeared to have struck out the side for the second inning in a row, but home plate umpire Ed Rapuano decided that another Escobar two-strike breaking offering to Aaron Rowand was a bit too high. Rowand walked two pitches later.

Then A.J. Pierzynski, everyone's favorite player, walked up to the plate.

Pierzynski rapped one back at Escobar that hit off the pitcher's back and rolled toward first base. What did Escobar do? Throw to first or tag Pierzynski as Pierzynski ran past him? Escobar did both. He tagged Pierzynski and then threw to Erstad at first, although the throw was late and Erstad didn't have full control of it anyway. But first base umpire Randy Marsh called Pierzynski out because of the Escobar phantom tag, and it appeared that the White Sox inning was over. No, no, it wasn't over. This was a play that involved A.J. Pierzynski, and any play that involved A.J. Pierzynski was never over quickly. Pierzynski pointed at Escobar, claiming Escobar never tagged him.

Ozzie Guillén came out and argued that Escobar had tagged Pierzynski with his pitching hand with the ball still in his glove. After conferring, the umpiring crew agreed with Guillén and Pierzynski. One more time, Pierzynski was awarded first base after an apparent out, although this time there was no doubt he belonged there.

Angels manager Mike Scioscia came out for a prolonged debate with the umpires. He had no case to make. All the television replays showed that Escobar had tagged Pierzynski with his bare hand. Angels fans weren't happy, but the umpires ended up with the right call without a replay. Just because it centered around Pierzynski didn't mean Pierzynski should be called out when he was safe. Escobar had made a bad play because of his indecision, and that was all there was to it.

While he was on the field, Scioscia decided to make a pitching change. He brought in his closer, Francisco Rodríguez. Rodríguez had picked up 45 saves in 2005 and saved the Angels' win in Game 1. But that night, he didn't look like the reliable closer he had been during the regular season.

17. Game Five

Rodríguez was falling all over the place, and his pitches were all over the place as well. He worked the count full to Joe Crede, and that turned out to be an important factor in the next play. Crede grounded the ball up the middle, and Adam Kennedy made a diving stop behind second. From his knees, Kennedy threw home, trying to nail a sliding Rowand. But with two out and a full count on Crede, Rowand had been running on the pitch. Rowand beat the throw rather easily. The White Sox led, 4–3.

Yet one more time, the White Sox scored with the help of just one hit. And that hit barely made it to the outfield. It couldn't be said that the Angels made the most of their hits, because they got so few of them.

The White Sox got two insurance runs in the ninth inning on a double off the right field wall by Konerko and a sacrifice fly by Rowand. Now, there were only three outs to go. Contreras came out for the ninth to attempt to be the fourth Sox starter to throw a complete game. He was approaching 120 pitches but didn't appear tired, and he was sharp. Everything he threw was a strike.

Darrin Erstad hit a high hopper to Uribe at short. Uribe made a good play as he had little time. His quick release got Erstad by a step. Bengie Molina was next. He reached down for a low pitch and drove it to center. Rowand made the catch look easy as he charged in to snare it. Casey Kotchman was the Angels' last chance. He bounced one to first base that short-hopped Konerko. Konerko was able to scoop the ball (he was a good defensive first baseman, for which he rarely got credit), and he had an easy, unassisted putout.

Contreras threw 114 pitches and became the fourth consecutive White Sox pitcher to throw a complete game. The White Sox were the second team to throw four consecutive complete games in a post-season series. Ironically, the 1907 Cubs were the other team to do it, in the World Series. The fourth consecutive complete game was an amazing fete considering the complete game has almost disappeared in today's game.

"We all wanted to go out and throw complete games," Jon Garland said in 2015. "I don't know if it was the inner competition, we definitely built off each other that year. It was fun to be part of that.

Section Two—Making History

Paul Konerko runs to José Contreras to celebrate clinching a long-awaited World Series berth. Konerko made the last putout for the White Sox in advancing to and in the post-season. Contreras had pitched the fourth consecutive complete game against the Angels in the ALCS. The White Sox bullpen pitched a grand total of two-thirds of an inning in the five-game series.

At some point in everybody's career you want to do that. To be a part of that pitching staff, it's something special."[1]

Could White Sox fans believe it? For the first time in 46 years and only the second time since the Black Sox scandal, the Chicago

17. Game Five

White Sox were going to the World Series. No one had predicted it. No one had expected it even as the team had remained in first place in the AL Central Division. Many feared some tragedy or bad luck would prevent it. But there were countless champagne showers after the game. It had to be true; it just took a small time for most people to believe it. Even the stunned Angels had to believe it.

18

♦ ♦ ♦

The Last World Series

Nineteen fifty-nine. Dwight Eisenhower was president. It was the height of the Cold War that many feared would turn hot with nuclear weapons turning the earth into ash. Even White Sox fans born after 1959 are familiar with the story of the Chicago air raid sirens going off on the night of September 22 after the White Sox clinched the pennant in Cleveland. Many feared that the United States was under attack from the Soviet Union, and those people were not reacting out of paranoia. Only three years later, the Americans and the Soviets came close to a nuclear confrontation over Russian nuclear weapons being deployed in Cuba. In time, there would be other close calls.

Chicago wasted no time celebrating. Many fans greeted the American League champions when their plane landed in the early hours of the 23rd at Midway Airport. A ticker tape parade followed the next day. Owner Bill Veeck basked in the limelight.

Nineteen fifty-nine was the first year the White Sox were not controlled by the Comiskey family. Veeck had wrestled that control away and put his stamp on the team. The next season came the "Monster" scoreboard in center field that shot off fireworks when a Sox player hit a home run. Names were put on the back of uniforms. Both moves were ridiculed, although many teams now shoot off fireworks with home runs, and names on uniforms help because Major League Baseball has expanded several times, and it's hard for the casual fan to know all the players even with a scorecard. Do fans now even use scorecards?

Veeck owned the White Sox until 1961, when he sold the team

18. The Last World Series

to Arthur Allyn. Because of World War II injuries, Veeck suffered with numerous health problems for the rest of his life, and his health was one reason he sold the team. Some fans don't give him credit for the 1959 pennant because he had bought the team in the spring of that year, and many think most of the team was already in place. He would also be criticized for trading young players Norm Cash, Johnny Callison, Earl Battey, and John Romano for veterans in an effort to repeat as American League champions in 1960.

The 1959 team was truly a small ball outfit. They hit only 97 homers. Their leading home run hitter was catcher Sherm Lollar, who knocked out 22. He also led in the RBI department with 84. During the 1950s, the White Sox were known as the "go-go" White Sox, a squad that won games with defense, pitching, and speed. They scratched out runs in a big park. During the 1950s, the White Sox had some excellent teams, but they couldn't get past the Yankees, who had a powerful lineup. In the 1950s, only one manager won a pennant who wasn't a Yankees manager: Al Lopez, who managed the pennant-winning Indians in 1954 and the White Sox at the end of the decade. Lopez finally saw the Sox win the Series in 2005 at age 97. He died four days later, no doubt leaving this earth a happy man.

The most memorable event of the 1959 Series occurred in the fifth inning of Game 2, when Dodgers second baseman Charlie Neal homered. A fan, who was trying to capture a souvenir, knocked a beer off the ledge of the left field wall. Poor White Sox outfielder Al Smith got a sudsy shower to add to the insult of the home run. Photos showed the beer pouring down like a small waterfall. Smith lowered his head in his beer-soaked uniform as embarrassment added to disappointment.

After winning Game 1, 11–0, the White Sox dropped the next three. They forced a Game 6 in Chicago by beating a young Sandy Koufax, 1–0, in Game 5. Koufax gave up five hits in seven innings, with the only run scored during a double play. A six-run fourth inning in Game 6 sealed the fate of the doomed White Sox fate as they closed out the Series with a 9–3 loss in Comiskey.

The White Sox had three consecutive 90-win seasons from 1963 to 1965, the only time in franchise history that they put three consecutive 90-wins seasons together, finishing in second place each year. Nineteen sixty-three and 1964 marked two more times they couldn't get past the Yankees. In 1965, the Twins won the pennant with 102 wins. The White Sox have never won more than 100 games in any season. Every one of these teams was better than the pennant winners of 1959, even though the 1959 team had three future Hall of Famers (Early Wynn, Nelson Fox, and Luis Aparicio).

After 1965, the team went on a steady decline. Milwaukee, Toronto, New Orleans, and Seattle were just a few destinations that were rumored as potential new locations for the franchise as the losses mounted and the Cubs took over the city. Owners John Allyn and Bill Veeck didn't have the resources to compete as a major league franchise. The team had its second worst year with 106 losses in 1970. The decade closed out with the humiliation of Disco Demolition in 1979.

But now, in 2005, in a stadium that was only 15 years old, the franchise with a history of disappointment, losing, and self-inflicted wounds had ended their fans' decades of frustrations. They were in the World Series, and they would win it just as they had won the division and the playoffs. They would combine luck and opportunistic play. They would become world champions.

19

♦ ♦ ♦

Houston Astros

The Houston Astros broke into Major League Baseball as an expansion team in 1962, when they entered the National League along with the infamous New York Mets. (The Mets lost 120 games in their maiden year.) Houston lost 96 games but finished in eighth place, one rung above the hapless Chicago Cubs, who lost 103 games.

The Astros were known as the Colt .45s during their first three seasons. Their jersey sported the word COLTS in large letters, with a Western-looking handgun underneath. The Colt .45s played in a makeshift stadium called Colt Stadium. It has been described as a horrible place for both players and fans. The mosquitoes were large and numerous, and the Southern heat was intense.

"Colt Stadium was arguably the worst major league ballpark used in the last 50 years," wrote Kevin Richard in a 2009 article for ballparkdigest.com. "Imagine playing outdoors in Houston in the summertime, and then imagine cramming 10,000 sweaty bodies into a temporary stadium—the perfect environment to attract thousands of mosquitos."[1] Richard added that the park didn't have an upper deck, so fans had no shade. Heat exhaustion was a problem and, according to Richard, 80 people had to be given medical attention during a 1962 doubleheader.

The Colt .45s became the Astros in 1965 when the Astrodome hosted its first game on April 9. It was an exhibition contest against the Yankees. Mickey Mantle hit the first Astrodome home run, but the Astros won, 2–1. The Astrodome would never be known as a hitter's ballpark.

Up until 2005, in some ways, the Astros had experienced a

Section Two—Making History

history like the White Sox. At the start of October 1980, Houston was in first place in the NL West. The Astros finished the regular season against the Dodgers with a three-game series in LA. The Dodgers were in second place, three games behind the Astros. One win would give Houston its first division title. The Astros were playing well coming into Los Angeles, having won six of their last seven games. One win seemed likely.

But the Astros lost three straight one-run games, which forced a one-game playoff right there in Los Angeles. Fortunately for Houston, starter Joe Niekro won his 20th game with a complete-game, 7–1 victory. The Astros captured their first division title although they had tried their best not to win it.

The Phillies were their opponent in the League Championship Series. Four of the five games went into extra innings. In Game 5 in Houston, the Astros led, 5–2, going into the eighth inning. Philadelphia broke through with a five-run inning against Nolan Ryan to take a 7–5 lead. The Astros answered with two runs in the bottom of the inning, but the Phillies pushed in a run in the top of the 10th. Houston lost in front of their hometown fans despite getting 14 hits. The Phillies went on and won the World Series.

Houston returned to the playoffs in 1986 and were matched against the Mets in the NLCS. New York had won 108 games in the regular season with the likes of Gary Carter, Keith Hernandez, Darryl Strawberry, and Dwight Gooden. The Mets were the favorites.

The Mets went into Game 6 ready to clinch despite two dominating performances by Astros ace Mike Scott. Scott won Game 1, 1–0, with a complete-game five-hitter. He struck out 14. He won Game 4 with another complete game, this time a three-hitter. The final score in another pitching duel was 3–1.

As with the White Sox in Game 4 of the ALCS in 1983, the Astros needed a strong performance from a left-hander. Seventeen-game winner Bob Knepper took the mound, and if he could help Houston win, the Astros could have Mike Scott ready for Game 7.

Knepper, like Britt Burns, pitched brilliantly. He took a 3–0 lead into the ninth inning, having given up only two hits. Hold the lead, and the Astros would be one win away from a World Series.

19. Houston Astros

But it wasn't meant to be. Knepper gave up a triple, single, and double, and the Mets were within one run. Houston brought in closer Dave Smith, who had command problems and walked Carter and Strawberry to load the bases. Ray Knight hit a sacrifice fly to right to tie the game.

The game went into extra innings and lasted almost five hours. New York scored three runs in the top of the 16th inning. The Astros tried to rally, scoring two runs in the bottom of the inning. But Kevin Bass struck out with the tying and winning runs on base.

There was no game seven. No Mike Scott. The Mets went to the World Series and beat the Red Sox in an improbable way. The curse for the long-suffering Red Sox and their fans continued. But, of course there is no such thing as a curse.

The Astros went to the playoffs in 1997, 1998, 1999, 2001, and 2004. They didn't advance to the NLCS until 2004. It appeared that Houston would finally go to the World Series when they took a 3–2 lead in the NLCS against St. Louis. But the Astros lost Games 6 and 7 in St. Louis and failed to make the World Series once more.

In early 2005, it looked like the Astros had no chance to go the post-season. On May 24, with a seven-game losing streak, Houston's record stood at 15–30. During the next 117 games, the Astros put on a series of winning streaks. They still needed a win in game 162 against the Cubs in Minute Maid Park. It didn't come easy. Houston led, 6–4, in the ninth inning, but with two outs, the Cubs had runners on second and third. Cubs second baseman José Macías hit a line drive off Brad Lidge that, if had been a little to the left or right, would have driven in the tying run. But it was right at Eric Bruntlett, who was playing second base in place of Craig Biggio. Bruntlett made the catch about chest high, and the Astros won an unlikely playoff spot, their second straight wild card berth.

Fast forward to the fifth game of the NLCS, once again against St. Louis. Brad Lidge was on the mound in his usual closing role in the top of the ninth. Houston led, 4–2. The Astros needed just one more win, and they were going to the World Series.

Things looked so good in the beginning. Lidge struck out John Rodriguez and John Mabry. Now only one out to go, but, as we all

Section Two—Making History

know, that last out can be so hard to get. David Eckstein singled to left. Jim Edmonds walked. Representing the go-ahead run, Albert Pujols stepped up to the plate. Of course, Pujols, owner of 41 homers in the regular season, was the last person Astros fans wanted to see in this situation. Still, there they stood, looking for that last out, that last, World Series-qualifying out.

Astros fans of that generation know what happened next. Using a massive swing, Pujols launched one that would have made NASA proud. The fans in the left field seats at Minute Maid Park looked straight up and over their shoulders. Getting a souvenir was out of the question. The shot cleared everything, including the train tracks high above the stands. It was bad enough the Astros' lead was gone, but it had happened in such a prodigious fashion. As the saying goes, the Pujols drive would have been a homer in any park, maybe even the Grand Canyon.

Astros fans went silent and slowly sat back down. There was still the bottom of the ninth, but that turned out to be a three-up, three-down affair. The series headed back to St. Louis for Game 6.

It had happened again. Still, after over 60 years and three stadiums, Houston fans waited for the World Series. The Mets, who entered the National League with them, had gone to four World Series. But not the Astros. Would the Pujols home run deflate them? Would the Cardinals, with ex–White Sox manager Tony LaRussa, go to the Fall Classic instead?

"Needless to say, I didn't feel great after that," Lidge told writer Josh Criswell in 2023. "Like 'what just happened?' I was a little shell shocked. I'd had a run of good games against the Cardinals up to that point, including the previous year in the post-season and some of this post-season. But when he hit that, it was hard to wrap your head around, hard to believe for a little bit. We were kind of collectively hanging our heads."[2]

Then there was the flight to St. Louis. The pilot had an announcement to make. "If you look off to your right, we can still see the Albert Pujols home run still flying by." According to Lidge, catcher Brad Ausmus was behind it all as he asked the pilot to help play the trick. Astros players laughed and loosened up some.[3]

19. Houston Astros

Game 6 in St. Louis worked out just fine for the Astros. Roy Oswalt pitched seven innings, giving up only a run on three hits. Houston led, 5–1, going into the last inning. This time, there were no late-inning heroics by the Cardinals. The Astros won, 5–1, and were on their way to their first World Series. It would have been nice to clinch at home, but a clinch is a clinch.

The Astros had come a long way from Colt Stadium with its eagle-sized mosquitos to the Astrodome to Minute Maid Park to finally making the Fall Classic. There was only one drawback. If they had won in Houston, 20-game-winner Oswalt would have been in position to start Game 1 of the World Series in Chicago.

It was just another break for the White Sox.

Section Three

The World Series

It was still hard to believe. I had to drive by what was then called U.S. Cellular Field on the way to work every day. There was a flashing road sign by the expressway giving information about the World Series. *The World Series?*

Yes, there was a World Series happening in Chicago, the first since 1959.

The only other World Series in Chicago since the end of World War II was in 1945 when the Cubs played the Detroit Tigers. No Cub fan could or can tell you anything about that the Series except for the disgruntled fan, his goat, and his curse.

And, of course, there is no such thing as a curse.

From first look, it appears that the White Sox dominated the Houston Astros with a four-game sweep in the 2005 World Series. That was definitely not the case. Every game was close, with the largest margin of victory being two runs (which happened twice). On two occasions, Houston came back to tie the game in the late innings. Also on two occasions, they had the tying run on base when they made their last out. The third game went 14 innings. The Astros made only two errors in the Series and basically made the White Sox earn everything they got.

Houston was no fluke team that lucked its way into the Series. After their bad 15–30 start, the Astros went 74–43. In the playoffs, they beat Atlanta, who, for a period of about 15 years, always made the post-season. They eliminated St. Louis, who had won 100 games in the regular season.

Eventually, two members of the 2005 Astros would be elected to the Hall of Fame. Craig Biggio was enshrined in 2015 and Jeff

Section Three—The World Series

Bagwell in 2017. (No one from the 2005 White Sox has been elected to the Hall, with the exception of Frank Thomas, who was injured most of the year. It doesn't look like anyone else will. Mark Buehrle is on the Hall of Fame ballot, but even he doesn't think he belongs there. Paul Konerko has 439 career home runs to go along 1,412 RBIs but he has not garnered much support.)

Houston's pitching staff boasted Roy Owalt, a 20-game winner in 2005. There was also Andy Pettitte, who would garner 256 wins in his career. Finally, there was Roger Clemens, who would have been elected to the Hall of Fame a long time ago if not for his alleged steroid use.

What the 2005 White Sox demonstrated is what it looks like when the players and manager are a perfect match. Ozzie Guillén wanted them to bunt, and they did. He wanted to move runners in other ways, and they did. He wanted them to be aggressive on the base paths, and they were. What were his expectations for defensive play? The author doesn't know, but they played a good defense. The White Sox didn't give runs away; in fact, they took them away.

Now the doubts and the worries about choking were gone. Manager Guillén put it in perspective to his team as they prepared for the Series. "Don't be satisfied just to be here," he told his players. "Win this thing. Win this thing."[1]

The 2005 World Series would show just how good the White Sox were. Perhaps they were not as good as the 1961 Yankees, who had Mickey Mantle and Roger Maris. Maybe not as good as the Oakland A's, who won three Series in a row in the early 1970s. Or maybe not as good as the Cincinnati Reds, who followed the A's with back-to-championships in 1975 and 1976, including a 7–0 post-season record in 1976. But the 2005 White Sox proved to be the best team in franchise history. There is no doubt about that.

20

❖ ❖ ❖

Game One

The 2005 World Series began in Chicago on October 22. It was a Saturday night game, and the weather was cool but not cold, at least in the first inning. The high for the day was 66 degrees, although the temperature dropped steadily as the game progressed.

José Contreras, who had become the staff ace, started for the White Sox. Roger Clemens, who had broken into baseball a year before Ozzie Guillén, was on the hill for the Astros. The first pitch of the game was a strike to Craig Biggio.

The game was scoreless in the bottom of the first inning with two outs and Jermaine Dye up. Dye battled Clemens for nine pitches, went with an outside fastball, and drove it to right field. The ball cleared the fence, and the first run of the Series crossed home plate.

Dye did what he and Konerko often did. Many times they didn't attempt to pull away pitches. This strategy often produced hits, many times extra-base this, and this time a home run. It was the way the White Sox played in 2005. Like a good NFL quarterback, they took what the opposition gave them.

The Astros tied it almost immediately. With one out in the second inning, Mike Lamb reached down for a sinking outside fastball and socked it to right-center. Rowand got a good jump on it, but all he could do was stand by the wall and watch it go into the first row. It was a nice piece of hitting by Lamb on a pretty good pitch.

In the bottom of the inning, the White Sox played small ball and scored on some aggressive baserunning, which had become their trademark during the 2005 season. Carl Everett led off with a soft single to center. Rowand executed the hit-and-run perfectly. He

Section Three—The World Series

tapped a ground ball toward the wide hole between first base and second as Everett took off. The ball barely made it into the outfield, but Rowand had a single, and Everett advanced to third. There were no outs.

Pierzynski followed with a hopper to Astros first baseman Lamb, who found himself in a quandary. He could just tag first, but that would allow Rowand to advance into scoring position. Instead, Lamb looked Everett back to third and threw to second for the force. Everett saw his chance. On the throw to second, he took off for the plate. He scored with a dive, and there was no throw. The Sox had a run the small-ball way again. Everett had strayed far from third. Should Lamb have thrown to third to get Everett? Maybe it was a case of a player having too many choices at once. Regardless, the White Sox led, 2–1.

It quickly became 3–1 when Juan Uribe hit a double that zipped into the left-center field gap, driving in Pierzynski. The Astros bounced right back in the third inning. With one out, Adam Everett and Biggio were on first and second. Willy Taveras, playing small ball, bunted toward third base. Contreras made an excellent play, bare-handing the ball and firing to first for the out. Taveras no doubt was going for a hit to load the bases, but he did succeed in moving runners to second and third.

Lance Berkman hit a two-run double that went screaming into the right field corner. Everett and Biggio easily scored, Berkman stood on second, and the game was tied, 3–3. But just think what might have happened if Contreras had not made that good play on the Taveras bunt. Three runs would have scored, the Astros would have been ahead, and there still would have been only one out. The potential for a big inning would have been there, and perhaps Houston would have gone on to win Game 1. Important plays like the Contreras throw happened often for the White Sox in 2005, and that was one reason they won so many games.

In the fourth inning, something got into Joe Crede again. Clemens, appearing to be injured, had left the game after two innings. Rookie left-hander Wandy Rodríguez was on the mound. Crede homered to left-center on which center fielder Taveras made a valiant

20. Game One

attempt to rob Crede with a well-timed leap at the wall. But the ball sailed a good five feet over his glove, and the White Sox led, 4–3.

Contreras settled down and had clean innings from the fourth through the sixth. But some of his pitches were tailing too far inside, and the Astros decided to take advantage of that in the seventh inning. Jeff Bagwell led off and was hit by a tailing pitch. He barely moved. He just let it glance off him, and he took a base. (His uniform was hurt more than he was.)

One out later, Brad Ausmus did the same thing. An inside pitch tailed in, and he let it glance off his jersey sleeve. It was obvious what the Astros were doing. Normally if a pitcher hit two batters in an inning, the opposition wouldn't be happy even if the pitches had been accidents. The Astros put two runners on without the benefit of a hit, walk, or error. It looked so easy as their hitters just stood there.

Everett's ground ball resulted in a force at second base. With men on first and third and two outs, Biggio knocked a grounder that looked like it was headed past third and down the line. Two runs would have scored. But wait. Something had gotten into Joe Crede again. He dove, snared the grounder, and threw Biggio out. The inning was over, and the White Sox still led. Oh, they still led because Crede had homered in the fourth inning.

In the 1970 World Series, Orioles third baseman Brooks Robinson made a number of great plays that frustrated the Cincinnati Reds. Robinson was considered by many to be the greatest defensive third baseman of all time. Crede can't be put in that same category, because he didn't play as long as Robinson. But his defense had been invaluable to the White Sox in the regular and post-seasons. His play against Biggio was only one indication of that. Only Robin Ventura could compete with Crede as the best White Sox defensive third basemen.

Then came the eighth inning, just another dramatic and memorable inning that the White Sox experienced that post-season. It must go down as something truly historic, and not just in White Sox history.

Willy Taveras opened the inning with a double off the base of the left-center field wall. That was it for José Contreras. For the first

Section Three—The World Series

time in 11 days and the first time since the ninth inning of the first game in the ALCS against the Angels, the White Sox used their bullpen. Neal Cotts, who had been used in that Game 1, came in again.

Lance Berkman lined a single to left. The White Sox caught another break because the ball was hit so hard, Taveras had to stop at third. The Sox were still ahead, but there were still no outs, and, once more, it appeared that Houston would break the game open. Morgan Ensberg, who had 36 homers and 101 RBI during the regular season, was next up. The right-handed hitting third baseman battled Cotts but struck out on a high fastball. One out. Left-handed and home run-hitting Mike Lamb followed. Lamb also struck out. He missed a nice pitch on the outside corner.

Now future Hall of Famer Jeff Bagwell stepped up. Ozzie Guillén strolled to the mound, patted Cotts on the back, and motioned to the bullpen for another reliever. Guillén pointed to his right arm and extended his arms high and wide. He was calling for the big guy, Bobby Jenks. It would be power against power. It would be Bobby Jenks, the guy who hadn't pitched a full season in the majors, against Jeff Bagwell, owner of 449 homers in his 15th season.

The equipment used by Fox Sports timed Jenks as throwing between 96 and 100 mph. On two occasions, it was clear that Jenks was overthrowing, as his 100 mph pitches sailed way high, and Pierzynski made two good plays in snaring them. if either one of those pitches got by Pierzynski, the game would have been tied. The pitches almost took Pierzynski's glove off.

Mark Gonzales, who covered the White Sox for the *Chicago Tribune*, described Jenks as "throwing aspirins."[1] Maybe the ball looked that small to Bagwell. Bagwell fouled pitches off and went to his knees with one swing. Finally, he struck out on a high-outside fastball that was clocked at 98 mph. Inning and threat over.

First and third and no one out for the Astros, and no one scored. Not much different from the game in Boston when the Red Sox had failed to score with none out and the bases loaded. It was another huge inning for the White Sox bullpen. U.S. Cellular was a wall of noise as Jenks walked off the mound with a celebratory gesture.

Pierzynski led off the bottom of the inning with a ground single

20. Game One

to right. He stayed on first as Crede and Uribe flied out. Then Pierzynski took a walking lead off first. Astros reliever Russ Springer, for some reason, was not paying attention. Why should he? Pierzynski had no stolen bases during the regular season. But after walking a few steps, Pierzynski took off running and wasn't challenged. He stole second base standing up. It was an A.J. Pierzynski type of play. He put himself in scoring position.

Scott Podsednik was at the plate. Center fielder Taveras was shifted to left-center. Ripping into a high-inside pitch, Podsednik hit a fly into the gap in right-center. It looked like he had slapped the ball into a black hole, as there wasn't an Astro in sight. Pierzynski, after his rare stolen base, was able to score easily. Podsednik ended up at third with a triple. The White Sox had an insurance run.

Jenks came out to close out the ninth inning. Jason Lane struck out. Brad Ausmus was completely jammed on another fastball and rolled out weakly to shortstop. Jenks started Adam Everett with a breaking pitch and struck him out. Jenks had faced four batters and struck out three. The White Sox won Game 1, 5–3. It was their first World Series win at home since 1959 and the second since 1919.

21

◆ ◆ ◆

Game Two

Game 2 of the 2005 World Series was odd. That's the best way to describe a contest when either team could have won. In the end, the Astros had to be talking to themselves, just as they had after the Pujols home run. But this one had to hurt more because it seemed as if events had conspired against them and for the White Sox. Just ask the Angels.

One more time, the White Sox got a big break. And they won it in the most improbable way.

The night of October 23 was cold and wet. One would think home runs unlikely, but the ball was still flying out of the ball park pretty well even with Mark Buehrle and Andy Pettitte on the mound.

Houston's Morgan Ensberg hit the first homer of the night in the top of the second inning. He lined a Mark Buehrle pitch into the left field seats. The cold air did nothing to stop the drive, as it was a no-doubt-about-it home run.

Then came the bottom of the second inning, a strange bottom of the second. But it was just another part of the unlikely White Sox post-season. With one out, Aaron Rowand rapped one right past Astros third baseman Ensberg. A hard-hit ball, but just a single. Then the strangeness began.

A.J. Pierzynski sent an opposite field drive to left. Astros left fielder Chris Burke had a hard time gauging the ball as he got to the fence. He never got close to making the catch, and it hit in the middle of the fence to Burke's right. Pierzynski should have had at least a double.

But wait ... for some reason, Rowand thought Burke was going

21. Game Two

to make the catch even though Burke had looked clueless. Rowand could only advance to second base. Pierzynski only got a single when he almost had a homer.

Things worked for the White Sox when Joe Crede dropped a single into right just a few feet off the line, scoring Rowand. But more strangeness happened.

Juan Uribe popped one up to short right field. Craig Biggio went back on the ball and camped under it. But the future Hall of Famer dropped it like a Little Leaguer. Pierzynski scampered home, and the White Sox had a 2–1 lead. Things like this only happened in a White Sox 2005 World Series.

The lead lasted one out. Willy Taveras continued his hot hitting when he lined one right the right field line. The speedy center fielder easily made it into third with a triple. He scored on a sacrifice fly by Lance Berkman, and the game was tied at 2–2.

Things looked good for the Astros going into the bottom of the seventh inning. They led, 4–2, on the strength of a two-run double by Berkman, who now had three RBI in the game. Andy Pettitte had left the game after six innings even though he was pitching well. But he gave up two hits in the sixth and was at the 98-pitch mark. Houston manager Phil Garner went to his bullpen and brought in Dan Wheeler. Things started well enough for Wheeler when Crede fouled out to third. But Uribe crushed one and smacked a double off the left-center field wall. Podsednik followed with a strikeout, and it appeared Wheeler would have a clean inning.

Break Number Five

However, Wheeler seemed to lose his command. He walked Iguchi on a full count. There was another full count on Dye. Wheeler threw a fast ball tailing in on Dye, and at first glance it looked like another walk. Home plate umpire Jeff Nelson motioned Dye to first, saying he had been hit by a pitch.

Dye hesitated briefly at the plate. He didn't know if the pitch hit him, but he gladly took the base Nelson was giving him. Perhaps Nelson just assumed it had hit Dye from the sound and the fact that

Section Three—The World Series

Wheeler was throwing the ball over the place. Regardless, the bases were loaded. "That was a pretty good at-bat for myself," Dye told NBC Sports Chicago writer Vinnie Duber almost 15 years later. "I'm fouling off tough pitches, he throws a ball up and in, and it just glances off my bat. I just took one step to first base because I really didn't know if it hit me or hit the bat, and then I realized it hit the bat. I turned and looked at the umpire, and he says, 'go to first base.' It was a tough call for the umpire. Everybody's human, everyone makes mistakes, but I think that was a turning point in our season and in that game."[2]

Fox Sports showed the replay of the pitch numerous times, and the ball clearly hit the bottom of the bat. Fox play-by-play man Joe Buck got more irritated with each replay. He compared it to the Pierzynski dropped third strike, when there was no comparison. Obviously, he didn't want the White Sox to win, or at least he gave that impression. Getting a break on an umpire's call is not cheating, despite Buck's insinuations.

Regardless of Buck's whining, the bases were loaded, and Paul Konerko walked up to the plate. Garner brought in right-hander Chad Qualls. History followed. Konerko took a healthy cut at the first Qualls offering. From the sound of the bat striking the ball and from the crowd roar, it looked like good things for the White Sox. Left fielder Burke came to an almost dead stop at the warning track because he knew it was gone. Because the night skies were even darker from the misty rain, it was easy to see the white ball against the black as it cleared the White Sox bullpen and flew well into the seats. *Grand slam.*

Konerko raised his fist triumphantly in the air as he rounded first base. As he neared second, the stadium fireworks brightened the darker sky. Rounding third, he saw his teammates waiting at the plate with congratulations. As he trotted toward the dugout, the crowd got louder. One older fan sitting two rows behind the dugout held up a little sign that read, "I've waited 92 years for this" (Joe Buck had ridiculed the fan when the cameras spotted him and his little sign earlier. Later, the man was caught sleeping. He was awake for the grand slam.) The fans kept cheering, and the noise heightened. The fans

21. Game Two

Konerko GS—Paul Konerko celebrates his seventh-inning grand slam against the Astros in Game Two of the World Series. It was the greatest moment in his career and will go down as the greatest moment in the history of the Chicago White Sox.

wanted Konerko to come out to tip his hat to the cheers. Konerko did that, and the noise increased. Fox color man Tim McCarver described the scene as "Bedlam in Chicago."

Nine years later, Konerko tipped his cap to cheering fans again. He was walking off the field on September 28, 2014. It was the last time he would be on the field, as he was retiring. He was surprised when he looked into the stands to see many fans with tears of sadness because he was leaving. The tears were also joyful as they remembered his career and his World Series grand slam home run, which stands as the greatest moment in the history of the Chicago White Sox.

Back to Game 2 of the 2005 World Series. Fire-balling Bobby Jenks was back on the mound for the ninth inning. But the Astros were not going down easily. Jeff Bagwell hit an outside fastball off the end of the bat, but he had the strength to get it into center field for a leadoff single. Jeff Lane swung at three Jenks fastballs. He missed

Section Three—The World Series

them all. One out. Chris Burke didn't offer at four Jenks pitches. They were all out of the strike zone. First and second.

Brad Ausmus was next, and he hit a slow roller to Konerko. The runners advanced to second and third, putting the tying run on second. But there were two outs. Things still looked good for Jenks and the White Sox, but this game wasn't over yet.

Sixteen-year veteran José Vizcaíno came out to pinch-hit. The switch-hitting infielder slapped a line drive past Juan Uribe into left field for a single. Bagwell easily scored, and Burke followed right behind him. Podsednik made a good throw, but it was a little to the first base side of home plate. Burke made an excellent slide around Pierzynski's attempted tag and swiped home with his left hand. The game was now tied, 6–6. Guillén pulled a distraught Jenks and replaced him with Neal Cotts. Cotts got Mike Lamb to send a routine fly to left field, and the inning was over.

Brad Lidge, the pitcher who gave up the Pujols moon shot, came out for the bottom of the ninth. Uribe hit a fly to left-center, and the crowd reacted as if it were a home run. No such luck. Center fielder Taveras caught it just short of the warning track. Podsednik was next. So history was made again.

Podsednik hit a 2–1 pitch. It was obvious that he had hit it well, but he had only one home run the entire season, and that was in the first game of the ALDS against the Red Sox. Now he had his second homer as the ball disappeared into the right-center field seats.

"How do things like this happen?" a clearly irritated Tim McCarver wondered. Who knows? But the White Sox had a 7–6 victory and a 2–0 lead in the World Series.

Did small ball contribute to the Podsednik home run? Did Lidge lay in a fastball because he didn't want to walk Podsednik, a base stealing threat? In the post-game interview with Chris Myers of Fox Sports, Podsednik said he was looking for fastballs during his entire at-bat. Perhaps Lidge just hoped Podsednik would just hit it at someone. Instead, he hit it out of the park.

During the June 14, 2024, post-game show on NBCSports Chicago, Podsednik said he had glanced in the dugout when the count was 2–0. Manager Guillén signaled to take the pitch because it was

21. Game Two

Scott Podsednik was looking for a fastball, and he got it. He hit it into the right-center field seats for a game-winning, walk-off home run in Game Two of the World Series. He had hit no home runs during the regular season. His teammates were somewhat surprised.

important for base-stealing threat Podsednik to get on base, Podsednik took a strike, and the home run came on the next pitch, giving Podsednik "a feeling I can't describe."

During the celebration at home plate, Guillén went out of his way to console Jenks. He didn't want to lose his closer because of a blown save. He gave Jenks a little pat on the cheek. "He told me to keep my chin up," Jenks told Chuck Garfien on the November 2, 2023, Win Trust Sox podcast. "You're going to be out there. Be ready."

Now it was on to Houston for the first World Series game ever played in the state of Texas.

22

♦ ♦ ♦

Game Three

Game 3 was an exhausting one for Astros fans. It lasted nearly six hours and, near its end, fans were yawing in their seats. It also had to be the most frustrating. Houston went out to a 4–0 lead, lost the lead, tied the game, and then failed to take advantage of numerous chances in the ninth and extra innings to score and win the game. They lost the game when the White Sox found an unlikely hero, a player who had not been on the team when the season began.

In fact, this was not a well-played game by the White Sox. They committed three errors and went nine straight innings without scoring a run. But just as in several other post-season games in 2005, they found a way to win.

The game started out in a normal way, at least for the Astros. Craig Biggio led off the Houston first with a double to the left-center field gap. He scored on Lance Berkman's opposite field single to left.

In the third inning, sloppy play by the White Sox led to two runs by the Astros. Adam Everett picked up an infield hit. Since the game was in a National League park, there was no DH, so pitcher Roy Oswalt stepped up to the plate. The Sox pitched out, and Pierzynski fired to first base in an attempt pick off a straying Everett. Everett got into a rundown but was able to get back to first when Uribe's throw to Konerko hit Everett in the back. Oswalt then did what he was intending to do in the beginning. He sacrificed Everett to second.

Biggio got his second hit of the game as he singled to right, scoring Everett. Biggio eventually scored on a single by Morgan Ensberg. The inning ended with a 3–0 Astros lead, and the runs were unearned. They were the first unearned runs given up by the White

22. Game Three

Sox during the post-season. Ozzie Guillén was not happy with the milestone. In the dugout, he flung a plastic bottle of water. Poor water bottle.

In the fourth inning, a big break went Houston's way. There is a strange ground rule in Minute Maid Park. A vertical yellow line separates the wall in left field from the wall in left-center. A few feet from the top of the wall, a line runs across the left-center field structure. If a drive hits to the left of the vertical line, it is still in play. If it hits to the right of the line and clears the other line going across, it is a home run.

Jason Lane hit a fly that appeared to be on the left-center field side, clearing the horizontal line. Second base umpire Gary Cederstrom immediately and emphatically called it a home run, and the Astros led, 4–0. But the Fox Sports replay showed it on the left field side (by inches), and it should have been in play. Regardless, in the end, it would make no difference in the game's outcome.

Joe Crede led off the fifth inning, and there was no doubt about his home run. His opposite field drive cleared the right field wall by a good distance, and the White Sox had their first run of the game. For Roy Oswalt and the Astros, things would only worsen.

Uribe followed with a single to left-center. Jon Garland tried to sacrifice Uribe over, failed, and struck out. But the hits kept coming for the White Sox. Podsednik singled to right. Tadahito Iguchi lined a single to center that scored Uribe. Dye battled Oswalt with an eight-pitch at-bat before he blooped a single to center, chasing Podsednik home.

At that time, Minute Maid had another strange feature. There was a small mound in deep center that ran up to the wall. A flagpole stood on the mound in fair territory, and center field was a 427-foot canyon. After Konerko flied out, Pierzynski walloped one into that canyon, driving in Iguchi and Dye. Now the White Sox led, 5–4.

But the Sox almost had an even bigger inning. They had loaded the bases with a Rowand walk and a Crede hit by a pitch. Uribe sent a high drive down the right field line that had enough distance for a home run. But it landed just foul, and the White Sox barely missed putting up a nine-run inning. Uribe flied to right to end the inning after he just missed a grand slam.

The Astros tied the game in the eighth inning on an RBI double by Lane. The Houston club didn't know it, but they had just scored their last run of the 2005 season.

The game went into extra innings, with each team failing to capitalize on scoring opportunities. Finally, there came the 14th inning, a strange inning that was indictive of the post-season the White Sox had.

Ezequiel Astacio was on the mound for Houston. Dye led off with a single. Konerko hit a shot down to third base. Morgan Ensberg made a fantastic defensive play when he snagged the ball on a short hop and threw to second to force Dye. The relay to first beat Konerko by a step. A potential double was turned into two outs, and it appeared Houston would come up in the bottom of the inning with another chance to win.

Geoff Blum, who had come into the game in the 13th inning to play second base, stepped up to the plate. Blum had been picked up in a trade with the Padres at the end of July. He had had 95 at-bats for the White Sox and hit one home run. He hit another one in Houston. Blum golfed a low-inside pitch, and his home run soared down the right field line, giving the White Sox a one-run lead. Astros manager Phil Garner threw a folding chair in the dugout. Poor folding chair.

The White Sox were not done scoring, and they picked up a run without hitting the ball more than 90 feet. Rowand tapped one toward third base for an infield hit when Ensberg decided not to challenge Rowand with a throw. Crede dribbled a slow roller to third. Ensberg let it go, hoping it would go foul. It didn't. In fact, it smacked the middle of the third base bag. The ball had been hit so softly that it only bounced a few inches off the base.

Astacio walked the next two hitters, forcing home an insurance run. Damaso Marte went out for his second inning of work. With two outs and a man on second, it appeared the White Sox would close out the game in non-dramatic fashion. But no, not this game.

Brad Ausmus hit a sharp grounder to shortstop, right at Uribe. It was a routine play normally, but Uribe bobbled the ball for his second

22. Game Three

error of the game. The winning run came to the plate in the person of Adam Everett.

Guillén decided to bring in Mark Buehrle to get the last out. It was the first relief appearance for Buehrle since the 2000 playoffs during his rookie year. It is the only known time that he came in to pitch with a beer buzz. The game ended quietly when Everett popped out to Uribe on the third pitch. The White Sox now had a commanding three games to nothing lead in the Series.

The game lasted exactly 5:41. Both teams left 15 runners on base. The Sox made three errors, which was not like them in 2005. The Astros got only one hit after the fourth inning and none during the extra innings. It was past one o'clock in the morning when the game finally ended, the longest in time consumed in World Series history. For the Astros, it was their sixth extra-inning loss in the post-season. They had won only once. Now they had to win four in a row or go home.

23

♦ ♦ ♦

Game Four

October 26, 2005, was a special day for the Chicago White Sox. For the first time since October 15, 1917, they were going into a game with a chance to win the World Series. In that 1917 game, they beat the New York Giants, 4–2, behind the complete-game pitching of Red Faber. Faber spent his entire 20-year career with the White Sox and won 254 games. He was elected to the Hall of Fame in 1964. The Giants, of course, now play in San Francisco, having moved to the West Coast in 1957, two years before the last White Sox World Series.

That Wednesday in 2005, the White Sox had Freddy García on the mound. The Astros countered with 10-game winner Brandon Backe. Backe pitched his heart out. He went seven innings giving up only five hits, striking out seven and walking no one. In six of the seven innings, he got the first two hitters out, making it very hard for the White Sox to score. They didn't.

By the sixth inning, the game was still scoreless, and the Astros mounted their biggest threat. With one out, Willy Taveras singled. Lance Berkman walked. Morgan Ensberg battled Garica, hitting a deep drive to left but pulling it foul. Ensberg worked the count full. On the 3–2 pitch, both Taveras and Berkman were running. Ensberg struck out, and Taveras and Bergman pulled off a double steal. Pierzynski wanted to make a throw but dropped the pitch.

Mike Lamb was next with two out. García tried to get Lamb to chase two low-outside pitches out of the zone, but Lamb took both. Lamb was then walked intentionally to load the bases. Jason Lane followed. When García threw a pitch in the dirt, and Pierzynski

23. Game Four

blocked it perfectly. Lane battled García, fouling off good pitches, but finally struck out on a high fastball to end the inning. García left the game after the seventh inning, giving up no runs and allowing only four hits.

Luckless Brad Lidge came on in the eighth inning. Willie Harris, pinch-hitting for García, slapped an opposite field, line drive single to left. Podsednik laid down a perfect bunt. He inched it out to Lidge, and the Astros pitcher had no choice but to go to first. Carl Everett, hitting for Iguchi, hit a sharp grounder to second to advance Harris to third base.

Jermaine Dye stepped up to the plate. Poor Brad Lidge. He made a good pitch on the outside part of the plate, and it had a nice downward movement. But Dye didn't try to do too much with it. He grounded it past Lidge and into center field for an RBI single. Harris trotted home with the game's first run.

This small ball was just another indication of why Ozzie Guillén was the right manager for the White Sox that year. He liked to play for one run, demanding that players go with his plan. The White Sox players believed in and executed that plan. They bunted and otherwise moved runners along. They didn't romp over the opposition; the White Sox won close games. When they needed power, they provided it.

The White Sox were six outs away from winning the World Series. Bobby Jenks was in again for the save in the ninth inning. As in the rest of the Series, it would not be easy.

That ninth inning was a typical Astros inning. Lane led off with a single and was advanced to second on a bunt by Ausmus. The tying run was in scoring position, and Chris Burke pinch-hit for Adam Everett, who had no RBI in the Series. Burke lifted a high foul down the third base line. Both Crede and Uribe chased it, with Uribe having the better angle. Uribe looked up and over, gauging where the seats were. He dove into the seats and made the catch. A frustrated Burke walked to the dugout. One out left.

Orlando Palmeiro was up next to pinch-hit for Brad Lidge. Jenks threw Palmeiro a breaking pitch, and he chopped it over the mound. Jenks made a lame leap for the bounding ball, but it bounced over his

Section Three—The World Series

Bobby Jenks celebrates closing out the Boston Red Sox. Jenks came out of nowhere to become the Sox closer. He saved the division clincher, the series clincher against Boston, and the deciding game of the 2005 World Series. At the time this book was written, Bobby Jenks was diagnosed with stomach cancer.

23. Game Four

head. Uribe darted in, picked it up on a bounce, and quickly fired it to first. Palmeiro was out by a half-step. The game was over. The Chicago White Sox were the 2005 World Series champions.

For the Astros, who played well for the most part, it had to be maddening. After taking a 4–0 lead in Game 3, they scored but one run in their last 19 innings. With the two home losses, they had lost three post-season games in a row in Houston. The team had come into the National League in 1962 with the Mets. The Mets had won two World Series, with the Astros having won none. Houston would finally win their first Series in 2017 after being moved to the American League in 2013. The Astros would eventually be accused of cheating, although it was a different type of cheating than the Black Sox. Ironically, it was the White Sox who caught them first.

As for the White Sox, the Series sweep gave them eight straight post-season wins. They lost only once, giving them a post season record of 11–1. Chicago also won their last five regular season games. The only post-season loss was the 3–2 setback to the Angels. Thus, the White Sox came within two runs of posting a 16-game winning streak.

The White Sox were often called the second team in the second city. The Cubs had a cult-like following that no other major league team possessed. They were lovable even when losing. At one time the Cubs were owned the Tribune Company, and the corporation used all is media operations to promote the franchise. The White Sox were drowned out by the noise. But it was the White Sox who finally ended the Chicago World Series drought.

Jermaine Dye was selected as the Series MVP, a good choice. However, any number of Sox players could have been given the recognition. Everyone on the team contributed during the post-season and the regular season was well. That is what makes a team truly great. Just ask Geoff Blum. Or even Willie Harris. The stars can't do everything.

The strategy used by GM Kenny Williams had worked. Change the face of the team and the type of play as well. Look at the post-season. Eight of the 11 games were decided by three runs or less. The White Sox found ways to win. They got the clutch RBI, and their pitching staff got the big outs. Just ask the Red Sox. Just ask the Angels. Just ask the Astros.

The 2005 championship soothed a lot of pain and helped many fans forget the bad seasons, the disappointing seasons, and the constant obstacles that seemed to get in their way. The White Sox had finally done it. They had risen to the top of the baseball world, and they had done it in a truly remarkable and memorable way. And, as we all know, there is no such thing as a curse.

Finally, for Sox CEO Jerry Reinsdorf, it was a vindication of sorts. After the controversies surrounding the 1994 strike and the 1997 White Flag Trade, his club became the first Chicago baseball team since 1917 to win the World Series. Paul Konerko kept the ball from the last out and presented it to Reinsdorf as a historic keepsake.

"I was stunned when Pauk Konerko presented me with the baseball from the final out of the World Series," Reinsdorf stated in an email in 2024. "It was totally unexpected. I have told people since that it was the most emotional moment of my professional life. It meant so much that a player understood my love for baseball, the city of Chicago, and all this ball represented to me. It is a piece of memorabilia I cherish most to this day."

24

♦ ♦ ♦

Aftermath

The beginning of the 2006 season gave the White Sox another first. For the first time since 1918, when Woodrow Wilson was President, the Sox began the season as defending world champions. It was a new experience for their fans, too. When did any current Sox fan ever speculate about their team repeating? Never. Not even the man who held the "I've waited 92 years for this" sign. He was five years old in 1918 and probably didn't even know who the Chicago White Sox were at the time.

After the victory parade, GM Ken Williams didn't sit on his hands. On November 25, in a somewhat surprising move, Williams sent center fielder Aaron Rowand to Philadelphia for Jim Thome. Rowand's defense had been so much a part of the 2005 success. But the White Sox had a young outfielder named Brian Anderson, and it was thought that he had the potential to take the place of Rowand. Thome could supply power from the left side of the plate since Carl Everett was granted free agency and went to Seattle.

The White Sox unveiled their World Series championship flag during Opening Day ceremonies on April 2, 2006. They beat the Cleveland Indians, 10–4.

There seemed to be a different aura around the White Sox. They lost four straight games after the opener, but later in the month went on an eight-game winning streak. April ended and May began with the Sox back in first place with an 18–7 record. Unlike other seasons, when fans waited for disaster or disappointment, it appeared that the White Sox just knew how to win. Going back to the end of the 2005 season, the post-season, and the first 25 games of the 2006 season, the Sox posted a record of 34–8.

Section Three—The World Series

On June 20, St. Louis came into with town for a three-game series with the second-best record in the National League. In game one, the White Sox annihilated the Cardinals, 20–4. The Sox poured it on with an 11-run third inning, when they sent 16 batters to the plate. They pounded out 24 hits. The next day, the Sox annihilated St. Louis again 13–5, this time pounding out 16 hits. They scored in each of the first five innings, which included four runs in the first inning and five runs in the second.

In the third game, the Sox picked up only one hit against Cardinals starter Anthony Reyes. That came in the seventh inning on a Jim Thome home run. They had only one other baserunner when Dye got on because of a Cardinals error. But the White Sox completed the sweep with a 1–0 win behind the eight-inning, one-hit pitching of Freddy Garica. Bobby Jenks got his 21st save with a three-up, three-down ninth inning. The Sox had dropped to second place, but they were only a half-game behind first-place Detroit, possessing the second-best record in the American League. As for Thome, he would hit another dramatic homer in another 1–0 game a little more than two years later.

Houston came in for a three-game series. Chicago won the first game, 7–4, as José Contreras improved his record to 8–0. In game two, it seemed like old times as the Sox came back from a 5–1 deficit to win, 6–5, in 10 innings. It gave them their sixth straight win over the Astros. Then came game three.

Houston led, 9–1, going into the bottom of the seventh inning. The White Sox scored one run in that frame and three more in the eighth. More Sox heroics came in the bottom of the ninth. With two outs, Tadahito Iguchi hit a game-tying grand slam over the left-center field fence. One could see the shoulders of Astros center fielder Willy Taveras sag as he watched the ball sail out of the ballpark. Not again, he had to be thinking. Houston couldn't win with a 9–1 lead? The White Sox were doing it to them again?

Taveras ended up getting the game-winning RBI in the 13th inning, driving in Adam Everett, who had led off the frame with a triple. This time Houston held on for a 10–9 win. They finally beat the White Sox, whose nine-game winning streak had snapped. But

24. Aftermath

Houston would not go to the post-season that year for the first time since 2003.

At the All-Star break on July 9, the White Sox still held down second place and still had the second-best record in the American League. From the start of 2005, the post-season, and the first half of 2006, the Sox were an amazing 167–95. It appeared that they would be defending their world championship in the post-season one way or another.

But it wasn't meant to be.

The American League Central was uncharacteristically strong in 2006. Both Detroit and Minnesota won more than 90 games. As the Sox went into their last home game of the season on September 24, they had already been eliminated from the division race and were on the verge of being eliminated as a wild card. The bittersweet game attracted 37,518 fans. The crowd came to say goodbye to 2006 and say thanks for the winning during the past two years.

The Sox offense exploded with five homers against the Mariners, which included two by Konerko and a grand slam by Uribe. But when Neal Cotts came in to mop things up in the eighth inning, he gave up back-to-back homers to Ben Broussard and Jose Lopez. Cotts, one of the World Series heroes the year before, was immediately taken out. His ERA had ballooned to over five for the season, and boos cascaded on him as he made his sad walk to the dugout. Once there, Cotts was in tears. A total of 91 batters had gotten on base in Cotts' 54 innings for the season. It was a tough year for him after being so dominant in 2005. It all meant a third-place finish for the White Sox.

The fans cheered their team when the Sox walked off the field with a 12–7 win. On the second to the last day of the season, the White Sox won their 90th game. It was the first time the team won 90 games in consecutive seasons in 40 years. But they still had not succeeded in getting consecutive first-place finishes or playoff berths in the history of the franchise.

Things had reverted to their great hitting but no championship years. The White Sox scored 868 runs and walloped 236 homers. They had three players over 100 RBI, including newcomer Thome. Yet

Section Three—The World Series

they went 38–45 during the last three months, and the season had to be looked upon as a disappointment. Once again, their fans were forced to say, "Wait 'til next year."

The White Sox played the Texas Rangers on a winter-like spring night on April 18, 2007. The temperature was a nippy 41 at the game's start. Players and fans could see their breath. Fans dressed in winter coats, sported gloves, and shivered. The White Sox came into the game with a three-game losing streak and 5–7 record. Mark Buehrle was on the mound for the White Sox, and Kevin Millwood pitched for the Rangers.

Jim Thome hit two homers. Jermaine Dye hit a grand slam in the fifth inning when he lined a shot into the White Sox bullpen. In the Rangers' second inning, Hank Blalock hit a deep fly to right. Dye went back up against the wall, reached up, and robbed Blalock of a home run. It helped that Dye is 6'4". A shorter player would have had a tough time making that catch.

To lead off the third inning, Ranger Jerry Hairston, Jr., hit a grounder that looked like it would scoot over third base and head down the left field line. But Joe Crede, looking like he did in the 2005 Series, dove and speared the ball as he landed right on third base. He one-hopped the throw to first, and Konerko scooped it up. Hairston was out as he dove head-first into the bag.

Hairston was incensed with the call and had to be restrained from going after first base umpire James Hoye. Hoye threw Hairston out of the game. Hairston's anger and antics were for nothing. Every replay showed he was out. Hoye had it right, and Hairston had it wrong. It would have helped Hairston to run right to the bag instead of going into his idiotic slide.

Sammy Sosa, spending his last year in baseball with Texas, walked with one out in the fifth inning. He was the first baserunner for the Rangers. Buehrle picked Sosa off, which marked the 48th time Buehrle had picked off a runner. Sosa hadn't been all that far off the bag, but Buehrle still nailed him. It was just another time when Sosa didn't have his head in the game.

Blalock got robbed again on the next play. His hard-hit grounder looked like it was going into right field for a single. But Tadahito

24. Aftermath

Iguchi dove and snared the ball in short right field. His throw got Blalock by a couple of steps.

The reason these plays have been described in such detail is that, going into the ninth inning, they were the closest the Rangers got to a hit. Sosa had been their only baserunner as the White Sox had built a 6–0 lead.

Buehrle came out to pitch the ninth inning. Matt Kata began the inning for Texas by looking at strike three. Buehrle painted the outside corner with a pitch no one could have hit. Nelson Cruz was next. Buehrle struck him out swinging on a pitch that broke in and down under Cruz's hands. The ball got away from A.J. Pierzynski, but the Sox catcher corralled it and threw Cruz out at first base. No one was going to reach first safely on a dropped third strike with Pierzynski behind the plate.

Rangers catcher Gerald Laird was next. He was jammed on another tough inside pitch by Buehrle. Laird tapped a slow roller to Joe Crede, the perfect White Sox defender to record the last out. Crede scooped the ball up nicely and made a perfect throw to Konerko. Mark Buehrle had his no-hitter.

During a post-game interview, a television reporter described the no-hitter as Buehrle's first. Buehrle would throw another one in his 16-year career.

It was the first White Sox no-hitter since Wilson Álvarez no-hit the Orioles in Baltimore in August 1991. It was the first no-hitter thrown by a White Sox pitcher in Chicago since Joe Horlen no-hit the Tigers on September 10, 1967. The time of the game was typical for Buehrle, 2:03.

There was a strange statistic in the game. A walk, of course, is not an official at-bat. Because the absent-minded Sosa was picked off, the box score showed that the Rangers accumulated just 26 at-bats. Because of the walk, there was no perfect game, but the Rangers never sent more than three men to the plate in any inning. With this, they left no one on base. They never threatened in the very least as most of the outs were either strikeouts or routine plays.

The 6–0 win was a reminder of the 2005 season. Of course, it was a well-pitched game, there was good defense, and the Sox had

Section Three—The World Series

an opportunistic offense, getting six runs on only seven hits. Yet, the Sox would not look anything like their World Series team that season. They lost 90 games in 2007, the most since their last-place finish in old Comiskey Park in 1989. Buehrle would win only 10 games, his lowest season total with the exception of his shortened first season in 2000, when he made only three starts. It was a hard fall with the memories of 2005 still fresh.

The next year would be better. It would also be memorable ... but strange.

On September 1, 2008, the White Sox were tied with the Twins for the lead in the AL Central as each team sported a 77–60 record. The Sox got bad news about their left fielder, Carlos Quentin. Unhappy with an unproductive at-bat, Quentin slammed his hand against his bat and broke his wrist. He was out for the season.

The Sox had acquired Quentin from the Diamondbacks. The young Quentin was in his third season and appeared on his way to a great career. At the time of his injury, the left fielder already had 36 homers and 100 RBI. Now, in the middle of tight division race, the Sox had a gaping hole in the middle of their lineup. Quentin would have some decent years, but he was never the same dominating hitter again.

As the month progressed, the Sox were in good shape. On September 23, they headed into Minnesota in first place, 2½ games ahead of the second-place Twins. The White Sox had never a great history of playing in the Humphrey Metrodome, and that bad play continued in the three-game series. The Twins won games one and two 9–3 and 3–2. In game three, it appeared that the Sox would escape Minneapolis with a win when they took a 6–1 lead in the top of the fourth inning. Minnesota tied it the eighth inning and won in the 10th. The Twins took over first place, with the White Sox a half-game back.

On the last day of the season, both the Twins and White Sox won. The half-game margin was still there because the Sox had to play Detroit in a make-up game for a rainout on September 13. The last-place Tigers would come to Chicago to complete their season in what was a meaningless game for them.

In the bottom of the sixth inning, White Sox rookie shortstop

24. Aftermath

Alexei Ramírez faced Tigers reliever Gary Glover with the score 2–2 and the bases loaded. Glover hung a breaking pitch, and Ramírez knocked it way into the left field seats for a grand slam. The slam was Ramírez's fourth, which tied the record for most grand slams by a rookie. The Sox went on to win, 8–2, setting up a tie-breaker with the Twins the next day.

The Twins, because of the Sox's horrid play in Minnesota, won the season series between the teams, 10–9. It made some sense that the tie-breaker would be played in Minnesota. But the league decided on a coin toss to determine home field advantage, and that toss happened two weeks before the season ended. With another piece of luck, the White Sox won the toss. Baseball is almost an impossible game to predict, and the Sox could have won a tie-breaker in Minnesota. However, it is safe to say the team was happy the game was played in Chicago, even if that meant beating three different teams on three consecutive days.

The tie-breaker against the Twins would become known to White Sox fans as the "Black Out" Game. The team encouraged fans to wear black to the park, and they were given black rally towels on entering the stadium. It was an effective promotion and added emotion to the contest.

For this game #163, it would be lefty John Danks for the Sox and righty Nick Blackburn for the Twins. Each had 11 wins for the season. The game began with more post-season White Sox luck. Denard Span led off the contest with a walk. The Twins called for a hit-and-run, and Alexi Casilla ripped into a Danks pitch, but his line drive was right at Juan Uribe, who was playing third base. Uribe threw across the diamond to Konerko for an easy double play. Joe Mauer struck out, and the Twins' first inning ended harmlessly and quickly.

The contest was still scoreless in the top of the fifth inning when Michael Cuddyer picked up the Twins' first hit, a double to left. Delmon Young flied out to center, and Cuddyer advanced to third. Brendan Harris lifted a fly to shallow center. Cuddyer broke for home, and Ken Griffey, Jr. uncorked a perfect throw home. The ball arrived on one bounce to Pierzynski, who held onto the ball even with Cuddyer running into him. Pierzynski took nothing for

Section Three—The World Series

granted. He turned and showed home plate umpire Tim McClelland that he had held onto the ball. Cuddyer was out by a few steps and never even touched home plate. The game remained scoreless.

On a ball hit that shallow, a runner usually doesn't attempt to go home. But in this case, one run could have meant a great deal, so the Twins took the risk. Additionally, Danks was pitching well. The Twins would not get another hit off Danks until the eighth inning, and that runner was wiped out on a double play. The Twins' gamble was worth it, even if it didn't turn out well for them.

Danks had pitched the game of his career in a big game, as Britt Burns had done 25 years earlier. Only Danks would not lose. Jim Thome provided the only run of the game. He led off the bottom of the seventh inning with a center field home run that disappeared way over the fence and somewhere into the night. Its distance was estimated at 461 feet, and Thome and Sox fans knew it was gone as soon as he hit it. The homer was his 34th of the season and one of 612 in his Hall of Fame career.

Bobby Jenks came in to close the game in the ninth. He began by striking out 20-home-run pinch-hitter Jason Kubel. Back to the top of the order and Denard Span. Span grounded out to Konerko. The luckless Alexi Casilla was the Twins' last chance. Jenks was able to jam Casilla, who hit a shallow fly to center. Brian Anderson, playing center field, had a long run but came in to make a diving catch. The White Sox had won their fifth division title. For the first time since 1906, both Chicago baseball teams were in the post-season. The Cubs had won their division with a National League-leading 97 wins on the 100th anniversary of their last world championship. Could this be an all–Chicago World Series?

No. The Cubs folded like a pretzel and were swept by Manny Ramirez and the Dodgers. They were outscored, 20–6, in the process.

The White Sox did only slightly better. They travelled to Tropicana Field to play the Rays. Attendance has never been great in Tampa, but the Rays were able to draw over 35,000 spectators in each game. (There was a comedian doing a skit that was shown on the Rays jumbotron. "I've been a Rays fan for a long time," he said. "Ever since June. No, July.") More importantly, the deeper Rays won both

24. Aftermath

games in Florida and eliminated the White Sox in four games. The Sox never had much of a chance in the series.

Even with some disappointment, the White Sox had accomplished a great deal from 2005 to 2008. There were two division titles and the World Series championship. They had another 90-win season and the excitement of Mark Buerhle's no-hitter. It was their most successful run in decades. Unfortunately, trouble was ahead.

25

♦ ♦ ♦

Decline

Thursday, July 23, 2009, appeared to be just another day and just another game on the schedule for the Chicago White Sox. In the majors, it is known as a "get-away day." Because the Sox were going on a road trip to Detroit and Minneapolis, the team was playing an afternoon game. Tampa provided the competition. The Rays were not duplicating their 2008 World Series season. They'd end up with 84 wins and out of the playoffs.

Mark Buehrle was on the mound. At that point, he was having a fine season, coming into the game with a 10–3 record. First baseman Josh Fields gave Buehrle a 4–0 lead with a grand slam in the second inning. That was more than Buehrle needed.

As the game progressed, the Rays were not close to getting a hit. They topped slow grounders, lifted lazy fly balls, or struck out. The Sox added another run, and the outcome seemed certain. The White Sox would win; the Rays would lose. Nothing special.

But there was one special thing: Going into the ninth inning, Mark Buehrle had a perfect game. DeWayne Wise went in to play center field, pushing Scott Podsednik to his more normal left field position. Left fielder Carlos Quentin stayed on the bench. Wise got into the action very fast.

Gabe Kapler led off for the Rays and hit what looked like a home run to left center. Wise gave chase, first glancing down at the warning track and then charging the wall. He went up slightly over the fence and pulled the ball back to the playing field. The ball looked like the proverbial snow cone in his glove. Wise juggled the ball as he came down and secured it in his bare left hand. He raised his hand to

25. Decline

Buehrle—Mark Buehrle going into the windup for the final pitch of his perfect game on July 23, 2009. Jason Bartlett would ground out to shortstop Alexei Ramírez. It was Buehrle's second no-hitter of his career. His perfect game was saved by center fielder DeWayne Wise, who scaled the left-center field wall on a drive hit by ninth-inning leadoff hitter Gabe Kapler. Wise leaped, juggled the ball, and secured it in his bare hand as he fell to the warning track. On that spot on the wall, there are two words painted for posterity: "The Catch."

show the umpire he had made the catch. Buehrle stared out at center field, not quite believing what he saw. He still had his perfect game. (Later, there were two words painted on the wall where Wise made his play: "The Catch.")

Michel Hernández was next, and he worked the count to three-and-one. Buehrle didn't change his style. No taking extra time. He got the ball back from catcher Ramon Castro (who had never caught Buehrle before) and quickly went into this windup. Hernández took a strike on the outside corner. Buehrle pulled the string on the next pitch, and Hernández waved at it for strike three.

Jason Bartlett was the 27th Ray to bat. No drama here. A weak ground ball to shortstop Alexei Ramírez, and Mark Buehrle had his perfect game.

Section Three—The World Series

During the post-game celebration, manager Ozzie Guillén pointed out something to Buehrle. The Rays players stood in front of their dugout and applauded Buehrle. The Sox left-hander tipped his hat to his classy opponents.

The time of the game was identical to Buehrle's first no-hitter: 2:03. Eric Cooper was the home plate umpire, as he had been in the other no-hitter. In both games, the opposition never sent more than three men to the plate in an inning. The Sox used the home run to win. In both games, the Sox hit a grand slam, and they made the most out of the few hits they did pick up. In both games, their defense shined.

The White Sox had a so-so record of 50–45 but were only one percentage point behind first-place Detroit. Yet they would not finish with a winning season. The Sox went 29–38 the rest of the season and finished in a disappointing third place.

As of this writing in 2024, the White Sox have not returned to the World Series. In addition, in 2024, the team was going into another rebuild even though the franchise didn't like to use that term. They suffered a franchise record 14-game losing streak. The possibility of the White Sox seriously contending to go deep into the post-season wasn't likely until at least past the 20th anniversary of the 2005 champions.

Still, the period from 2005 through 2008 has to be looked upon as a great success. There were two division titles, another 90-win season, and milestone games like Mark Buehrle's no-hitters. The team provided plenty of memories and finally overcame history to make some lasting accomplishments.

But two players who made deep and everlasting contributions to White Sox history were Paul Konerko and Mark Buehrle. The Sox 2–1 win over Seattle on April 16, 2005, illustrates this.

It may sound strange, but the case can be made that Buehrle pitched the best game of his career that day, a game that was even better than his two no-hitters. The only Mariner to get a hit that day was Ichiro Suzuki. Suzuki's first hit was a blooper to center. His sixth-inning hit was a bleeding-heart grounder that barely made it into right field. Finally, in the ninth inning, Suzuki bounced a high

25. Decline

hopper past a diving Konerko and down the right field line. A fan interfered with the ball, but Suzuki was awarded a triple since it was deemed that he would have made it to third if the ball had stayed in play. It was a little surprising that Konerko wasn't guarding the line with the Sox only ahead by two runs late in the game.

Buehrle stuck out a career-high 12 and walked only one. There was a hard ball hit here and there, but the other Mariners, with one exception, never got close to a hit. As my description indicates, Suzuki's hits were not hit all that hard. Buehrle truly looked masterful.

The two White Sox runs? Two Paul Konerko home runs. The first baseman also made a diving stab of a grounder in the ninth inning. He flipped to Buehrle covering first to get a key out and help ice the win.

Buehrle and Konerko. They were not just good players, each of them also provided a real identity to the White Sox. Buehrle was not an overpowering pitcher, but he was always good for double-digit wins and kept his team in games while going at least seven innings. Konerko, seen as a quiet leader, was consistently able to put up good power numbers every season.

In other words, each player did his job. Their fans appreciated them for their efforts and contributions, and they were good drawing cards. Both will be remembered for generations to come. In a sense, during the early 2000s, they were the Chicago White Sox.

26

♦ ♦ ♦

Legacies

As of this writing, Ozzie Guillén is still a White Sox legend of sorts. In addition to still being the only White Sox manager to win a World Series in more than 100 years, he is one of only two Sox managers to win two division titles since divisional play began in 1969. (Tony LaRussa is the other, with titles in 1983 and 2021.) Yet he left his position in 2011 at the end of a disappointing season with a cloud hanging over his head.

During an angry rant after a late May 2011 loss in Toronto, Guillén described an odd image of people urinating on the statues that stand on the outfield concourse at Guaranteed Rate Field. Many fans thought that Guillén was accusing the fans of showing this lack of respect. Guillén likes to speak his mind, but this was one time he offended the wrong people.

Guillén had been talking during a pre-game press conference. ESPN blog writer Doug Padilla stated that Guillén was being misunderstood and that this was no attack on fans. "Around the 11-minute mark of his talk with reporters Sunday," Padilla wrote, "Guillén mentions TV shows and radio shows. From then on, he uses words like 'they' and 'people' to refer to what he is talking about, never once indicating that he is talking about White Sox fans."[1]

Perhaps Padilla was right. Here is the most important part of the pre-game interview:

> Are they going to feel sorry for you if we're going to get fired. No. They only remember the 2005 team. In 2020 when we come here in a wheelchair, oh yeah, thank you. As soon as you leave the ballpark, they don't care about you anymore. They don't. The monuments, the statues they have for you when they pee on it when they are drunk. That's what they do. Oh, god, thank you

26. Legacies

for coming for 30 minutes for all the suffering you did all your life in and day out.[2]

This was part of an incoherent rant. No mention of fans here. But who are the people who are urinating on the monuments? If Guillén was misunderstood here, it was his fault. Didn't he remember how the "We don't owe the fans anything" remark went over? All I knew was that I only saw the monuments being treated with reverence. I talked about them with my daughter. I have seen other parents do the same.

The rant happened toward the end of May. Adam Dunn, a big off-season free agent signing, was hitting next to nothing. The White Sox were six wins under .500. Two thousand and five was still fresh in fans' minds, but it was slowly fading into the past. Guillén wasn't making sense and only provided a gross image. Some say Guillén liked to take pressure off his players by diverting attention to himself. If this was the strategy in this case, it didn't work.

The season was a huge letdown. Adam Dunn hit .159, and the White Sox ended up 16 games out of first place. The 2005 championship truly seemed like something that happened long ago.

Guillén left his White Sox manager's job just before the season ended in September. It was a messy affair. Guillén wanted a contract extension from the White Sox, but the team wasn't willing. Guillén left the team with two games left and signed a four-year deal with the Miami Marlins. The Marlins were set to open a new stadium in 2012 and looked forward to what they thought would be a contending season in front of large crowds.

Since Guillén was still under contract with the White Sox when he left for Florida, the Marlins sent Jhan Mariñez and Osvaldo Martínez to the White Sox as compensation. It was a strange kind of trade. Fans felt betrayed that Guillén had left before the season ended regardless of what he meant by his "peeing" statement. Fans also felt a deep disappointment since they had thought the Sox would turn into a consistent contender after 2005. But this was the third losing season since the championship.

Guillén had been the third base coach with the Marlins during their 2003 World Series title year and said he felt he was coming home. It appeared to be an exciting match. Then Guillén decided to

Section Three—The World Series

praise Fidel Castro in a *Time* magazine story. "I love Fidel Castro," Guillén was quoted in *Time*. "I respect Fidel Castro. A lot of people have wanted to kill Fidel Castro for the last 60 years but that [expletive] is still there."[3]

Praise for Castro would always be controversial, but this is America, and everyone can have a stated opinion. If Guillén had still been the manager of the White Sox, this would have caused a stir, but backlash would have passed after a short time. People would have said Ozzie was just being Ozzie, and that would have been the end of it.

But Guillén was now the manager of the Miami Marlins. Southern Florida is a hot-bed of Castro hate. So much happened after Castro took over Cuba, including a near-nuclear confrontation. Many Cubans who fled to America remained bitter that their country was taken away from them, and they were violently angry that the United States had not done enough to get rid of the Cuban dictator. Guillén was acting as if he didn't know this history and had no idea what backlash was coming his way. This would not be Ozzie just being Ozzie.

Guillén was forced to make a public apology and was suspended by the Marlins for five days. Guillén still defended himself, pointing out that President Obama was making moves with regards to normalizing relations with Cuba. Guillén had a point, and world views do change with the passage of time, even in Southern Florida. But there were still many people in the Miami area who had no use for anyone showing the slightest objectivity when it came to Fidel Castro. This was one time Guillén's outspokenness truly sabotaged him.

Even worse for Guillén, the Marlins had an awful season. The team ended up last in the NL East, losing 93 games. Guillén still had three years left on his managerial contract, but the Marlins fired him and ate the contract. Guillén hasn't managed in the major leagues since.

From 2012 through 2019, the White Sox only had one winning season, 2012. As the losses mounted, some fans hoped that Guillén would return to manage the team. Eventually he was interviewed for the job after Tony LaRussa was fired following the 2022 season, but Pedro Grifol got the job.

26. Legacies

Guillén is and has been a TV analyst for NBC Sports Chicago doing pre- and post-game analysis. For some reason, during a broadcast in 2023, Guillén said he "hated Nick Swisher with my heart."[4] Swisher played one season for the Sox in 2008. He hit for a low average but also hit 24 home runs. Swisher is hardly ever talked about by the Sox fan base for the obvious reason that he wasn't around for long. Why Guillén felt he had to say this nasty thing is hard to understand. He said Swisher is a phony, but even if he is, what does that have to do with the current White Sox situation?

Guillén still is a lightning rod. He spoke at the 2023 Society for American Baseball Research's national convention held at Palmer House Hotel in Chicago. Convention attendees were abuzz, knowing that Guillén had just entered the building. He spoke in front of a packed ballroom with his TV partner, Chuck Garfien. The room reacted strongly when Guillén said some complimentary things about Sammy Sosa. From appearances, he enjoyed getting instant feedback from the fans, and they enjoyed him.

Many of those fans still hope he returns to manage the White Sox with his "tell it like it is" style. His name will always be connected to the White Sox, and he will generate a variety of emotions. But until the team wins another World Series, Ozzie Guillén will hold a special place in franchise history, whether people are offended by him or not.

At the 2015 SoxFest fan convention, the team observed the 10th anniversary of the 2005 championship. At the media session, there were a handful of 2005 players. Aaron Rowand. Jon Garland. Geoff Blum. Tadahito Iguchi. But no Ozzie Guillén.

Guillén wasn't even in the country at the time of this SoxFest. He no doubt didn't want to face the backlash of his leaving in 2011 regardless of any plans he had at the time. Fans still like his "tell it like it is" style during NBC Sports shows, but it is not likely he will manage the White Sox even if some fans still fantasize about that possibility.

Like many other White Sox employees, GM Kenny Williams worked for the club for a long time. It began for Williams when the team selected him in the third round of the amateur draft in June

Section Three—The World Series

1982. His first full year as a player with the White Sox was in 1987, and that was his best major league season. He had 110 hits, including 11 home runs, and posted an average of .281. Williams bounced around, playing for Detroit, Toronto, and Montreal. His last major league game was on October 4, 1991.

Williams joined the White Sox as a scout in 1992. In 1995, he was promoted to director of minor league operations. Two years later, he was given the title vice-president of player development. Williams finally was named general manager, replacing Ron Schueler in late October 2000. Fans admired Williams' "going for it" way of doing things. Championships were so rare for Chicago baseball teams that there was little patience for youth movements. His aggressive move of trading for David Wells didn't work out, but the White Sox faithful liked the thought process. Win now, and worry about the future later.

Williams had to be affected by the disappointing play of the White Sox in 2003. They again finished second in 2004, but that result was somewhat deceiving. Despite scoring 865 runs, the Sox won three fewer games than the previous season and ended up nine games behind the Twins. Finishing behind the Twins again had to be frustrating.

Then came the big roster changes of 2005. Even sometime nemesis Ozzie Guillén gave Williams credit for the World Series win. "Kenny should be Executive of the Year because Kenny made more of a difference than we did. I think nobody gives him credit. They gave it to some guy in Cleveland. I don't know why."[5]

After the 2005 season, Williams didn't sit on his hands. On November 25, Williams, in a move that surprised some, traded center fielder Aaron Rowand to the Phillies for Jim Thome. The Sox needed left-handed power, and Thome gave it them. In 2006, Thome hit 42 homers and drove in 109 runs.

Part of the reasoning in trading a center fielder like Rowand was that the team had a young Brian Anderson ready to step into the role. But the 24-year-old Anderson wasn't quite ready. Anderson hit .225 in 2006 and was never an impact player despite his talent. He finished his career with Boston in 2009. Despite hitting 236

26. Legacies

homers in 2006, the team was unable to defend its championship in the post-season.

Williams made another aggressive move in late 2010 when he signed power-hitting Adam Dunn. But Dunn had the worst season of his career in 2011, hitting but 11 homers and putting up an average of .159. The deflated White Sox finished third. (At one point, Dunn was 3-for-53 against left-handed pitchers. In one night game, he hit a single to right against a lefty. Starting from the right field corner and working around the stadium like a wave, the fans gave Dunn a standing ovation. The good-natured Dunn tipped his helmet to the derisive cheers.)

After Ozzie Guillén left for Miami in 2011, Williams did an odd thing. He hired Robin Ventura to take over the managerial duties. The hire was intriguing to fans at first because of Ventura's great play with the White Sox during the 1990s. But Ventura had no managerial or coaching experience at the major league level. The Sox did well in 2012 under Ventura, winning 85 games and finishing only three games out of first place when not much was expected from the team. But Ventura would resign in 2016 after the four straight losing seasons, including a 99-loss year in 2013. At that time, 2013 was the worst season for the franchise in more than 40 years.

By this time, Williams had been moved up to executive vice president, and Rick Hahn had taken over as general manager. During the middle of the 2010s, the White Sox decided to go on a rebuilding program, and Williams helped engineer a trade that sent talented left-hander Chris Sale to the Red Sox for Michael Kopech, Yoan Moncada, and Alexander Basabe. Moncada was rated as one of the top prospects in baseball at the time of the trade.

During the Covid-19 pandemic-shortened season of 2020, the White Sox began showing signs that the rebuilding was taking shape. In the August 21 night game against the Cubs in Wrigley Field, the Sox won, 10–1, by hitting six home runs. During that season, fans did not attend games. These home runs looked even more majestic as they hit deep into the empty bleachers and ricocheted way back onto the field. Young and upcoming new stars Luis Robert, Jr. and Eloy Jiménez hit homers that dreary-looking night. Jiménez's drive was an estimated 466 feet.

Section Three—The World Series

For the first time since 2008, the White Sox made the post-season in 2020. They lost a best-of-three series against the A's in Oakland. But it appeared that the team was on the rise and would be contenders in 2021. In the first quarter of 2021, it looked like the Sox could return to the World Series. At the 40-game mark under new and returning manager Tony LaRussa, the White Sox were 25–15. Many were calling the Sox the best team in the American League. But then came some strangeness on May 17 in Minnesota.

The Sox were pounding the Twins, 15–4, going to the ninth inning. Minnesota decided to put catcher Willians Astudillo to pitch the ninth. Lobbing the ball up there, Astudillo was able to get the first two hitters. He then went 3–0 on Sox second-year catcher Yermin Mercedes. Mercedes swung on the 3–0 pitch and hit a center field homer. The meaningless run made it 16–4.

Manager LaRussa was not happy. He didn't want his team pouring it on and thought Mercedes shouldn't have swung at the 3–0 pitch. The next night, in the seventh inning, Twins pitcher Tyler Duffey threw behind Mercedes on the first pitch. Home plate umpire Jim Reynolds threw Duffey out of the game for retaliation. Twins manager Rocco Baldelli was also thrown out when he argued about the ejection of Duffey. LaRussa was not bothered by an opposing pitcher throwing behind one of his players.

The White Sox won 93 games that season and took their first division title in 13 years. Yet the team didn't seem the same after the Mercedes incident. Houston beat the Sox in four games in the opening Division Series. In their losing effort, the Sox were outscored, 25–6. They lost the last game at home, 10–1, and some thought they had given up.

By 2023, it was evident that the rebuild had failed. The Sox finished a dead even 81–81 in 2022 and self-destructed during the start of 2023. Coming off a 7–21 start, they would lose 101 games for the season, the most losses since the 1970 team, and third-most in franchise history.

In late August 2023, Williams and GM Rick Hahn were fired. Williams' tenure with the White Sox that spanned over five decades had ended. During his time in the front office as GM and executive

26. Legacies

vice president, the White Sox had four 90-win seasons, four division titles, one wild card berth, and one World Series championship. However, the 2010s was the first decade since the 1970s in which the White Sox did not go to the post-season. The team suffered eight losing seasons from 2010 to 2019. As a result, the Kenny Williams legacy is a mixed one, although 2005 can't be taken away from him.

Some fans wonder if Jerry Reinsdorf is concerned about his legacy. Does he worry what fans will say about him once he is gone? He oversaw the building of the new Comiskey Park, now known as Guaranteed Rate Field. There is also the United Center, housing his Bulls and the Black Hawks.

The White Sox were the first to reach 2,000,000 in attendance in Chicago. There has been a string of talented players who graced the Sox uniform. There is the 2005 World Series. Of course, there are also six NBA championships during the 1990s, when the Bulls twice won three championships in a row. No other Chicago major league franchise has won three consecutive championships. The Cubs won two, back in 1907–1908.

However, there was also the 1994 strike and the 1997 White Flag Trade. The Bulls have not been to the NBA Finals in over a quarter of a century. And there is the very high upper deck in Guaranteed Rate Field.

Technically, Jerry Reinsdorf is not the owner of the White Sox. He is the Chief Executive Officer who controls the majority of the stock. Regardless, he has run the franchise for a longer period than any one person. He has had his supporters, but his critics have been loud. Many have urged him to sell the franchise. But selling the team is something he will not do.

Some critics say he is too greedy, but many employees say he is loyal and generous. As time went on, he has become somewhat reclusive. He rarely gives interviews, and when he does, there are often strict conditions. When I attempted to interview him for my first book, I was told I would get 15 minutes. But the interview never happened.

What can Jerry Reinsdorf's legacy be? How about a new stadium?

The 2023 season went beyond disappointing. The team played

Section Three—The World Series

badly for the majority of the season, as the 101 losses indicate. In the aftermath, Jerry Reinsdorf visited the office of the mayor of Nashville during the winter meetings there. Were the Sox interested in relocating to Nashville? In February 2024, as his team began spring training in warm Arizona, Reinsdorf travelled to cold Springfield, Illinois, to lobby legislators for public funding for the stadium that would be located about two miles from the current site.

Fans do forget teams as time passes. But a new stadium would be a constant physical reminder of the man who ran the White Sox for decades. In the many times a fan would sit in the ballpark, he or she would eventually think of the man responsible for its existence.

Yes, Jerry Reinsdorf will have a legacy. It will be one of accomplishments and setbacks. And it will be one that will be hotly debated.

27

❖ ❖ ❖

Final

On December 8, 1985, the 12–1 Chicago Bears played the Indianapolis Colts. The dream of an undefeated season came unraveled the week before when Dan Marino picked apart the Bears "46" defense with 31 points in the first half and won a Monday night game in Miami, 38–24. In the first half against the Colts, the Bears looked lackluster in a 3–3 tie. Bears fans, used to seeing their team dismantle just about everyone, began booing as the Bears went into the locker room.

CBS TV announcers Don Criqui and Bob Trumpy were stunned. The Bears had all but locked up home field advantage in the playoffs, had only one loss, and were getting booed? What kind of fans did they have?

The boos were not of derision. They were boos of panic and the fear that another Chicago team would let them down. Fans worried that the Bears had peaked too soon and would not carry the winning momentum into the playoffs. The White Sox should have gone to the World Series in 1983 and didn't. The Cubs should have gone to the World Series in 1984 and didn't. The Black Hawks had a 2–0 lead in the seventh game of the NHL Stanley Cup Finals in 1971 and lost. No Chicago sports team had won a world championship since 1963. Would the 1985 Bears just add to that list?

The Bears outscored their opposition in three playoff games, 91–10, and won Super Bowl XX on January 26, 1986. Their relieved fans came out in frigid temperatures to watch the victory parade. After all, it was "Bear Weather."

This gripping fan fear confronted the White Sox in September

2005. It made no difference that the Bulls had won all those championships in the 1990s or that the Bears won the Super Bowl. This was Chicago baseball. Chicago baseball teams didn't win championships. They blew opportunities.

In examining the press coverage and recalling the last few weeks of the 2005 season, I found it amazing that the White Sox were functioning at all. An unbelievably hot Cleveland team was right behind them and gaining almost every day. As Cleveland turned it on, there were only more nightmares of Chicago baseball losses. Other teams had folded big-time, and would the White Sox join their ranks?

There were other doubts, too. Was Cleveland just the better team? Should the White Sox have done more at the trading deadline? Were the Sox plainly in for a downfall after their great start?

Aaron Rowand told me in 2015 as the team observed the tenth anniversary of the world championship that the players didn't pay attention to all the outside noise or what WSCR-670 personality Dan Bernstein described as "White Sox angst."[1] I'm sure that Rowand remembers things that way. However, the noise, the history, and the angst had to have an effect. Baseball players are human, and anyone can feel the pressure of expectations.

All of this merely made the accomplishments of the 2005 White Sox even more impressive. Winning at the major league level is difficult enough without having to deal with constant distractions that can only add to the pressure.

The 2005 White Sox. They overcame history. And then they made it.

Addendum

*Roland Hemond,
the Man Who Saved the Sox*

In 1968, the White Sox believed they were pennant contenders. The 1967 team finished three games out of first place in a four-team race. The Sox lost their last five games of the season because of a light-hitting team. In the off-season, they acquired two-time National League batting champion Tommy Davis. They also brought back Luis Aparicio, who they thought would be a potent leadoff hitter. At the beginning of the last year of pre-divisional play, the organization advertised itself to its fan base as a team destined for the World Series.

The start of the Major League Baseball season was delayed due to social unrest after the assassination of Martin Luther King, Jr. on April 4. The White Sox finally had their home and season opener on April 10 against Cleveland. The game turned out to be a disaster and a portend of a bad and disappointing season to come.

In 1968, Comiskey Park was regarded as being in a "bad neighborhood." With the violence following the King murder, many feared going the opener. Only 7,756 people showed up to see the game. To make matters worse, the White Sox played a horrible game. Fly balls were played into triples, their ace from the previous season gave up five runs in five innings, Tommy Davis went hitless in four at-bats, and the rest of the Sox offense was held to two singles. Cleveland won, 9–0.

The Sox lost the next nine games. Dating back to the end of the 1967 season, they had a 15-game losing streak. They finished with 95 losses, which was their worst showing since 1948, when they dropped

Addendum

101 games. A once greatly anticipated season turned into a devastating letdown.

Both leagues added two teams in 1969, and divisional play began. The White Sox were placed in the newly formed American League West with expansion teams Kansas City and Seattle. They finished in between the two first-year teams, one game behind Kansas City and only four ahead of last-place Seattle. The Sox drew poorly, failing to reach 10,000 fans for a game after September 1.

Things truly bottomed out in 1970. The White Sox lost 106 games. The future of the franchise was in jeopardy. The fan base had tuned out. (In May, there was a headline in the *Chicago Sun-Times* proclaiming that the team had drawn a little over 18,000 for a doubleheader. Yes, a crowd of 18,000 actually made news. They lost the doubleheader, and most crowds after that didn't approach 18,000.)

In September, owner John Allyn fired GM Ed Short and manager Don Gutteridge. Chuck Tanner became the new manager, and Roland Hemond was named General Manager. Both came from the Angels organization. The small, glasses-wearing man must be considered one of the most influential front office men in White Sox franchise history.

"It [the White Sox situation] was drawn as a dismal picture to me," Hemond told me in January 2000. "I was told by numerous people that it was a hopeless situation. They said, 'They're not drawing, financially they're not in a good position at all, and you're going into a difficult task.' There were others that were saying there were no good prospects in the organization. But I was young and excited about undertaking the job, so it didn't bother me to hear those things."[1]

The youthful Hemond got to work at the winter meetings in December 1970. He made three trades in less than 24 hours that involved 16 players. In the early spring, he acquired Pat Kelly from Kansas City, who turned out to be a good leadoff man and base stealer. The Chicago sports media took notice, Maybe the 1971 White Sox might not be that bad. In fact, they would be pretty good.

The White Sox began their season on the road that year. They were scheduled to play the Oakland A's, who had Bert Campaneris, Reggie Jackson, Catfish Hunter, and Sal Bando. The A's, which had won 89 games in 1970, were the favorites to win the AL West in 1971.

Doubleheaders were commonplace in the early 1970s. A's owner Charlie Finley, who liked to do different things, decided to open his team's season with two games instead of one. Not a bad idea, especially since the 1970 White Sox had lost a ton of doubleheaders. The favored A's could start their season with some real momentum.

But a strange thing happened. The White Sox, the team that Roland Hemond had been warned about, swept the doubleheader. The Sox fell behind, 4–0, in game one but won, 6–5. In game two, Chicago knocked out 13 hits and romped over Oakland, 12–4. They hit three homers. They would have had four, but a home run was taken away from left fielder Carlos May. On coming home, he missed the plate because he was too busy high-fiving a teammate instead of looking down. The A's noticed the mistake, tagged the plate, and May's home run became a triple. It didn't matter. The White Sox didn't need the run. Who wants an unlucky 13 total anyway?

Third baseman Bill Melton hit a home run in each game. In the second game, the home run was a grand slam. When talking to me about this years later, he asked, "Did I do this?"[2] Yes, Bill, you did that. The 1971 White Sox did this.

The team came home to Chicago, and new manager Chuck Tanner was interviewed on Chicago television. The interview took place right by the Chicago River, and Tanner looked like he had been part of the Chicago landscape for years. His optimism about his team had a hypnotic effect.

The home opener in 1970 drew just 11,473 fans. In 1969, it was about the same, and, of course, there was the minuscule opening crowd in 1968. The Sox front office hoped the 1971 opener could draw around 25,000.

A friend and I attended the game and sat down the left field line. Just before the game began, I looked behind me. Not an empty seat anywhere. I looked across the right field line. Same thing. I scanned the upper decks. Fans were everywhere. The hope had been for 25,000. The Sox got 43,253.

In my time as a fan, I have been to many games. I have been to

Addendum

playoff games, have seen a near no-hitter and walk-off wins. I've been in attendance during all the division title-winning seasons. Never, not at either stadium, was there the noise and emotion that engulfed Comiskey Park on April 9, 1971. When young Sox pitcher Tom Bradley (whom Hemond acquired from the Angels) struck out future Hall of Famer Harmon Killebrew with a high fastball in the sixth inning, the noise echoed around Comiskey. There hadn't been this kind of excitement in the old stadium for years.

The White Sox won the game, 3–2, in the ninth inning on a pinch-hit, line drive single by a guy named Rich McKinney. Comiskey Park erupted again. Several hundred fans ran onto the field. Not having expected such a crowd, White Sox security could do nothing to stop them. However, unlike the Disco Demolition crowd, these fans did nothing to damage the field. They slid into bases. In the outfield, they ran and ran. Back and forth, in circles, they ran and ran. You would have thought the White Sox had won the World Series instead of going 3–0 in a new season.

Fans didn't want to leave. On the concourses under the stands, fans yelled and yelled with joy and high-fived each other. The cheerful noise was deafening in an exhilarating way. There's nothing like a little hope.

Although 1971 was not a championship year, it was still a great season. The team won 23 more games than the previous year. Attendance could have been better, but it still improved by over 300,000.

There were personal milestones. Wilbur Wood, who had been a relief pitcher his whole career, was converted into a starter and won 22 games. Bill Melton became the first White Sox player to win a home run championship when he homered on the last day of the season. The White Sox began to look like a real baseball team.

Now that the White Sox were improving, Hemond made one of the most aggressive moves any Sox GM ever made. In December 1971, he traded left-handed pitcher Tommy John to the Los Angeles Dodgers for Richie Allen.

Allen was a talented but troubled player. He began his career in Philadelphia, where he won National League Rookie of the Year honors in 1964, Despite his talent, Allen was not popular with the fans in Philadelphia for various reasons (some racial). He began wearing a batting helmet when playing in the field because objects were thrown at him. One night, using his cleats, Allen carved the word "BOO" in giant letters in the infield dirt by his first base position. By the end of the 1969 season, Phillie fans were counting off the days until Allen left.

The Phillies traded Allen to St. Louis, and after one productive season there, the Cardinals sent him to the Dodgers. Now, he became a member of the White Sox.

Fans were happy with the trade, but also worried about Allen playing for his fourth team in four years. These worries persisted when Allen skipped spring training and didn't sign his contract with the Sox until right before the season started. Why was he skipping spring training? Oh, and Allen let it be known that he wanted to be called "Dick" and not "Richie."

A labor lockout delayed the start off the season, and the White Sox didn't play their first game until April 15 in Kansas City. In the ninth inning, with the game still scoreless, Allen led off with a massive home run to left-center. It was truly a demonstration of just how good Dick Allen was. But he cemented his relationship with Sox fans about six weeks later.

On June 4, the White Sox played a Sunday doubleheader against the Yankees. It was Bat Day at Comiskey Park, where kids were given free bats, and that promotion always drew a good crowd. But just under 52,000 people showed up, and it had been a long time since the Sox drew a crowd like that, attractive promotion or not.

Behind the brilliant pitching of Tom Bradley, the White Sox won game one, 6–1. Bill Melton, who had gotten off to a bad start, hit a towering home run in the fifth inning, and he began to look like the home run champion of the previous season. The second-place White Sox looked like contenders.

The crowd was deflated some when the second game lineups were announced. Dick Allen was not playing. Mike Andrews, usually a second baseman, had been inserted into Allen's spot, playing first base. It made no sense. The White Sox had drawn their largest crowd

Addendum

in memory, and Dick Allen wasn't playing in game two? He wasn't hurt, so why was he not in the lineup? Was the guy who had skipped spring training being given the star treatment?

In the bottom of the ninth inning, the Sox trailed, 4–2. They got two runners on base with one out. And who popped out of the dugout to pinch-hit? Dick Allen.

The crowd had thinned by the early evening, but fans went wild when they saw Allen's number 15. As for Allen, he slowly strode to the plate and readied himself to hit. He didn't show any indication that he was moved by the fan excitement or the importance of the moment. Just another day at the office.

The Yankees had brought in their closer, Sparky Lyle. His first pitch was a ball, a low offering. Using his powerful down-cutting motion, Allen swung at the next pitch. He whacked a low line drive that barely cleared the shortstop's head. At first, it looked like one of those hard-hit balls that gets caught by the outfielder. But the ball kept rising. Left fielder Roy White was going back, not coming in. He stopped at the wall and looked up. The line drive, which never got very high, zipped into the seats for a game-winning homer. Such dramatics hadn't happened at Comiskey for some time. Usually, it was the Yankees who won in the late innings.

At the end of the day, Sox fans allowed themselves to dream of a possible division title. However, a couple of weeks later, third baseman Bill Melton held a press conference to announce that he was out for the season. He needed back surgery due to an injury suffered when he fell off of his garage roof. During his meeting with reporters, Melton was in such pain that his voice was breaking.[3]

A few weeks later, Hemond picked up third baseman Ed Spiezio from the Padres. On August 12, Spiezio hit a two-run homer off Rollie Fingers in the 11th inning that helped the Sox beat the A's, 3–1, in Oakland.

It was an amazing game. Wilbur Wood pitched an 11-inning complete game and surrendered only two hits. Both were by right fielder Brant Alyea. It was Wood's 20th win of the season, his second consecutive 20-win season. Only Jim Kaat and Jack McDowell have had consecutive 20-win seasons for the Sox since 1972. Kaat accomplished that feat in 1974–1975, and McDowell did it in 1992–1993. (Hemond had picked Kaat up on waivers in August 1973.)

With Wood's win, the White Sox crawled past Oakland to move into first place by a percentage point. It was the first time the Sox had been in first place that late in the season since 1967.

Dick Allen won the American League MVP Award in this successful year. But the A's had too much depth and too much talent, and they won the AL West and the World Series. However, the Sox won 87 games and could have broken the 90-win barrier, but eight games had been knocked off the schedule due to the labor lockout. The White Sox would not win a division title for another 11 years.

Yet there were other positives. In two years, the White Sox went from 56 to 87 wins and from an attendance of 495,000 to 1.2 million. In 1972, Hemond was named Executive of the Year by *The Sporting News.* He would also win that award in 1989 as GM of the Orioles.

The truth is that the franchise was hanging by a thread in late 1970. Vast Comiskey Park was nothing but a wilderness of empty seats. The stadium was losing its sense of history and vitality and resembled a ghost town. If something hadn't been done quickly to improve things, it is very likely that owner John Allyn would have had to find a buyer for the team. It is also likely that the team would have left Chicago, leaving old Comiskey Park dark and empty. A charter member of the American League would have had to go on to other homes because of a losing team and waning fan base. A tradition would have been lost. Roland Hemond helped save that tradition.

Hemond left the White Sox after the 1985 season. He returned in 2001 as an executive advisor to GM Kenny Williams. His baseball career spanned 65 years. He must be looked upon as one of the most influential White Sox front office executives.

During the early 2000s, I secured a booth at SoxFest to sell two of my earlier Sox books. Leo Bauby, a collector of baseball photographs (he has thousands), shared the booth with me. Roland Hemond came by to have a look. Bauby reached for a photo of a boy who was about nine years old. The boy was wearing a cowboy hat that was so large that it concealed the boy's face. Hemond asked who the boy was.

Addendum

"Roland," Bauby said, "he's your son."

Hemond immediately reached for his wallet to purchase the photo. Bauby told Hemond to just take the photo without paying. Emotionally overwhelmed, Hemond walked away without a word and with tears in his eyes. Bauby had helped him retrieve a lost memory.

Roland Hemond. Good baseball man who helped keep the White Sox in Chicago. No doubt a good father. Roland Hemond. Just a good man.

Chapter Notes

Introduction

1. Charles Billington, *Comiskey Park's Last World Series: A History of the 1959 White Sox* (Jefferson, NC: McFarland, 2019), 183.

Chapter 1

1. "Dybzinski Won't Beef About Cut," *Chicago Tribune,* August 9, 2021.
2. Author telephone interview, July 2009.
3. Rebelo Kristena, "Durham's 1984 Error Revisited," *UPI,* October 8, 1991.
4. Phil Rogers, *Say It's So* (Chicago: Triumph Books, 2006), 74.

Chapter 2

1. Ron Brow, "Rally Cry no more Wait til next year," *Northwest Indiana Times,* October 4, 1983, Sec. D, 1.
2. Ron Brow, "Orioles Beat Sox at Own Game," *Northwest Indiana Times,* October 9, 1983, Sec, F, 2.

Chapter 3

1. Dan Helpingstine, *Through Hope and Despair: A Fan's Memories of the Chicago White Sox 1967–1997,* Self-Published, 2001, 2.
2. "Sox Bench Jocks Can't Forget Stewart," *Chicago Tribune,* August 10, 2021 (updated).
3. Matt Flesch, prod., *Last Comiskey—Story of the 1990 White Sox and the Final Season at Comiskey Park,* 2023.

4. Stew Thornley, "July 1, 1990—Andy Hawkins No-Hitter is No Winner for Yankees," *Society for American Baseball Research,* 2017.
5. Dan Helpingstine, *Through Hope and Despair: A Fan's Memories of the Chicago White Sox 1967–1997,* Self-Published, 2001, 161.

Chapter 4

1. Dan Helpingstine, *The Chicago White Sox—1959 and Beyond* (Charleston, SC: Arcadia, 2004), 77.
2. *Ibid.*

Chapter 5

1. https://www.treatavn.com/.
2. Rhiannon Walker, "The Day the White Sox took a chance on Bo Jackson," *Rememberwhedsdays,* April 5, 2017.
3. Major League Films, *Good Guys and Winners Wear Black-1993 Division Champion Chicago White Sox,* 1994.
4. Dan Helpingstine, *Chicago White Sox—1959 and Beyond* (Charleston, SC: Arcadia, 2004), 28.
5. *Ibid.,* 29.
6. "White Sox, Blue Jays Both Clinch; Chicago Wins West Crown for the First Time since 1983; Toronto Wraps Up Third Consecutive AL East Title," *Los Angeles Times Archive,* September 28, 1993.

Chapter 6

1. "Baseball / Daily Report: Status Quo Now Appeals to Reindsorf," *Los*

Chapter Notes

Angeles Times, August 1, 1994, online L.A. Times Archives.
2. Sridhar Pappu, "Sell Us the Sox," *Chicago Reader*, September 17, 1998, online article.
3. Murray Chass, "Owners Terminate Season, Without the World Series," *New York Times*, September 15, 1994.
4. John Logan, "Permanent Replacement and End of Labor's Only True Weapon," *International Labor and Working-Class History* 74 (Fall 2008): 171–192.
5. Mike Digiovanna, "MLB 1994 Strike: Replacement Players Provided Comic Relief, Farcical Baseball," *Los Angeles Times*, August 12, 2019.
6. *Ibid.*
7. *Ibid.*
8. Hannah Keyser, "A Look Back at Fan Rage From the 1994 Strike and Those Who Never Really Came Back," *Yahoo Sports.com*, August 12, 2009.
9. Phil Rogers, "1993 White Sox Reunion. A Run to a Division Title—and Memories for a Lifetime," *Chicago Tribune*, July 14, 2018.

Chapter 7

1. Paul Sullivan, "Cubs Virtual White Flag Trade on 2024 Season—Puts Heat on President Hoyer," *Chicago Tribune*, July 24, 2024.
2. Dan Helpingstine, *Through Hope and Despair*, 216.
3. Sridhar Pappu, "Sell Us the Sox," *Chicago Reader*, September 17, 1998, online article.

Chapter 8

1. Dan Helpingstine, *Chicago White Sox—1959 and Beyond*, 105–106.
2. *Ibid.*

Chapter 9

1. Peter Gammons, "Blue Jays Trade Wells to White Sox," ESPN.com, January 24, 2001.
2. *Ibid.*

3. Paul Sullivan, "Buyer Beware," *Chicago Tribune*, March 8, 2001, online.
4. Tom Dakers, "Today in Blue Jays History: Trade David Wells for Mike Sirotka," bluebirdbanter.com, January 14, 2023.
5. Chris Jaffe, "10th Anniversary of David Wells. Most Asinine Moment," fangraphs.com, May 3, 2011.

Chapter 10

1. "New Sox Promo Puts North Siders on Spot," *Chicago Tribune*, June 15, 2004.
2. Terrt Greenstein, "Sickening Start to Series," *Chicago Tribune*, September 17, 2003, Sec. 4, 1.
3. Rick Morrissey, "For Twins, Winning Tops Talent," *Chicago Tribune*, September 19, 2003, Sec. 4, 3.
4. *Ibid.*
5. *Ibid.*
6. Phil Rogers, "No Post Season, No Manuel," *Chicago Tribune*, September 18, 2003.

Chapter 11

1. Ozzie Guillén interview, May 14, 1999.
2. *Ibid.*
3. Phil Rogers, *Say It's So*, 43.

Chapter 12

1. Interview with author, February 2023.
2. Al Yellon, "Major League Predictions," bleedcubbieblue.com, April 3, 2005.
3. John Paschall, "One Decade Later, 2005 White Sox Remember Team More Than Individuals," NBC Sports, July 15, 2015.
4. Dave Van Dyck, "Manager Fumes after Sox Lose Series to worst team in Majors," *Chicago Tribune*, September 16, 2005.
5. Yellon, "Major League Predictions," bleedcubbieblue.com.
6. Rick Morrissey, "Choke no, Wob-

bling to Finish Certainly," *Chicago Tribune,* September 21, 2005, Sec. 4, 1.
  7. *Ibid.*

Chapter 13

  1. Sean Deveney, *The Original Curse: Did the Cubs Throw the 1918 World Series to Babe Ruth's Red Sox and Incite the Black Sox Scandal?* (New York: McGraw-Hill, 2009), 214.

Chapter 14

  1. Legends Program, October 18, 2018.

Chapter 17

  1. Doug Padilla, "In their words: The 2005 White Sox," *ESPN,* July 17, 2015, online.

Chapter 19

  1. Kevin Richard, "Colt Stadium, Houston Colt 45s, 1962–64," Ballparkdigest.com, April 4, 2009.
  2. Josh Criswell, "Brad Lidge Shares Hilarious Story from Infamous Pujols HR," Chron.com, September 19, 2023.
  3. *Ibid.*

Section Three: Introduction

  1. Major League Baseball Productions, *Chicago White Sox World Series Film,* 2005.

Chapter 20

  1. Interview with the author, February 2023.

Chapter 22

  2. Vinnie Duber, "Jermaine Dye's Surprising Revelation About Game 2 of the 2005 World Series," NBCSportsChicago.com.

Chapter 26

  1. Doug Padilla, "Fans Weren't Object of Ozzie's Ire," ESPN.com, May 30, 2011.
  2. *Ibid.*
  3. Oindrila Chowdhury, "When Ozzie Guillén Invited Trouble After Openly Praising a Dictator," Sportskeeda.com, December 13, 2022.
  4. "Ozzie Guillén calls Nick Swisher 'fake': 'I hate [him] with my heart,'" *Chicago Sun-Times,* August 6, 2020.
  5. Major League Baseball Productions, 2005 Chicago White Sox World Series Film, 2005.

Chapter 27

  1. *Boers and Bernstein* program, date unavailable.

Addendum

  1. Hemond interview, January 2000.
  2. Interview with author, January 1999.
  3. "Melton Lost for Season—Rare Back Season Treatment," *New York Times,* July 28, 1972, online.

Bibliography

Billington, Charles. *Comiskey Park's Last World Series—A History of the 1959 Chicago White Sox*. Jefferson, NC: McFarland, 2019.
Deveney, Sean. *The Original Curse: Did the Cubs Throw the 1918 World Series to Babe Ruth's Red Sox and Incite the Black Sox Scandal*. New York: McGraw-Hill, 2009.
Diamond, Jared. *Swing Kings—The Inside Story of Baseball's Home Run Revolution*. New York: Willam Morrow, 2020.
Freedman, Lew. *Early Wynn, The Go-Go White Sox and the 1959 World Series*. Jefferson, NC: McFarland, 2009.
Helpingstine, Dan. *The Chicago White Sox—1959 and Beyond*. Charleston, SC: Arcadia, 2004.
_____. *Through Hope and Despair—A Fan's Memories of the Chicago White Sox, 1967–1997*. Self-Published, 2001.
Rogers, Phil. *Say It's So: The Chicago White Sox's Magical Season*. Chicago: Triumph Books, 2006.

Films

Einhorn, Jeff, prod. *Winning Ugly 20 Years Later*, 2003.
Flesch, Matt. *Last Comiskey—Story of the 1990 White Sox and the Final Season at Comiskey Park*, 2023.
Major League Baseball Productions. *Good Guys and Winners Wear Black—1993 Division Champion Chicago White Sox*, 1994.
Major League Baseball Productions. *2005 Chicago White Sox World Series Film*, 2005.
Nike. *Bob Knows Bo—Pro Baseball*, 1991.

Newspapers and Magazines

Chicago Reader
Chicago Sun-Times
Chicago Tribune
Dayton Daily News
Gary Post-Tribune
Los Angeles Times
Minneapolis Star Tribune
New York Times
Northwest Indiana Times (Munster, IN)
Time Magazine

Web Sites

Ballparkdigest.com
Bleedcubbieblue.com
Bluebanter.com
CBS Sports
Chrom.com
ESPN.com
Fangaphs.com
Fox Sports
NBC Sports Chicago
TV and Radio Media

Bibliography

WGN-Television Chicago
Whitesoxinterative.com
Win Trust Sox Podcast
WMAQ-AM 670 Chicago

WMVP-AM 10000 Chicago
WSCR-AM 670 Chicago
Yahoo Sports
YouTube

Index

Allen, Dick 51, 52, 193, 194, 195
Allyn, Arthur 25, 135
Allyn, John 4, 13, 190, 195
Alomar, Roberto 82, 93
Alomar, Sandy 93
Alou, Moisés 10
Álvarez, Wilson 39, 40, 47, 59, 62, 64, 66, 93, 169
Alyea, Brant 194
Anderson, Brian 165, 172, 182
Angelos, Peter 57
Aparicio, Luis 2, 87, 136, 189
Ash, Gordon 76–78
Astacio, Ezequiel 158
Ausmus, Brad 140, 147, 149, 154, 158

Bagwell, Jeff 144, 147, 148, 153
Baines, Harold 2, 14, 19, 20, 22, 39
Baldwin, James 70
Bando, Sal 190
Bannister, Floyd 14
Barfield, Jesse 30
Bartlet, Jason 115
Bartman, Steve 10, 85, 128
Basabe, Alexander 183
Bass, Kevin 179
Battey, Earl 135
Bavasi, Bill 57
Bell, George 93
Belle, Albert 61, 93
Bensinger, Graham 93
Bere, Jason 53
Bergman, Lance 146, 148, 156, 160
Berman, Chris 110, 111, 116
Berra, Yogi 30
Berroa, Ángel 104
Berry, Ken .109
Biggio, Craig 143, 146, 147, 151, 156
Billingron, Charles 2
"Black Cat" 7, 10, 12, 32
Black Sox 3

"Black Wednesday" 5, 12, 48
"Blackout Game" 171
Blowers, Mike 29
Blum, Geoff 105, 158, 163, 181
Boddicker, Mike 17, 19
Boldelli, Rocco 184
Boyer, Brooks 81, 85
Bradley, Tom 192, 193
Break Number One 109
Break Number Two 111–112
Break Number Three 119–120
Break Number Four 125
Break Number Five 151–152
Brett, George 17, 27
Brock, Lou 61
Broglio, Ernie 61, 129
Broussard, Ben 167
Brunansky, Tom 34
Bruntlett, Eric 139
Buck, Joe 119, 152
Buckner, Bill 112
Buehrle, Mark 79, 93, 97, 99, 100, 118, 144, 150, 159, 168, 169, 174, 175, 176
Buhner, Jay 73
Bumbry, Al 19
Burke, Chris 150, 152, 154, 161
Burks, Ellis 49, 93
Burns, Britt 20, 23, 139, 172
Byrd, Paul 128

Cabrera, Orlando 123, 125
Calderón, Iván 30
Callison, Johnny 135
Cameron, Mike 74, 77
Campaneris, Bert 190
Canseco, José 27
Carlson, Mark 93
Carrasquel, Chico 87
Carter, Gary 138
Caruso, Mike 65
Castillo, Julio 10

203

Index

Castro, Fidel 180
"The Catch" 175
Cianchetti, Matt 71
Clemens, Roger 12, 82, 144, 145
Clement, Matt 71, 72, 107
Colon, Bartolo 83, 84, 93
Colt 45s 137
Colt Stadium 137
Contreras, José 104, 107, 108, 118, 128, 126–129, 132, 146, 147, 151, 166
Cooper, Eric 176
Cora, Joey 49
Cotts, Neal 148. 154, 167
Crede, Joe 84, 93, 101, 102, 104, 108, 110, 115, 119, 120, 126, 129, 131 146, 147, 151, 157, 168, 169
Cruz, Devvi 69
Cruz, Julio 2, 8, 16, 18, 21, 22
Cruz, Nelson 109
Cuddyer, Michael 83, 171
Curse in Reverse 112–116
"Curse of the Billy Goat" 5

Damon, Johnny 112, 113, 114, 115, 119
Darwin, Danny 62
Deer, Rob 36
Dempsey, Rick 21
Deveney, Sean 106, 107
DiGiovanna, Mike 57
DiMaggio, Joe 30
"Disco Demolition" 3, 156, 192
Donnelly, Brendan 123
Dotson, Richard 8, 18, 19, 48
Drew, J.D. 99
Duber, Vinnie 152
Durham, Ray 9, 10, 64–65, 67, 73, 93
Dwyer, Jim 19
Dybzinski, Jerry 8, 21, 109
Dye, Jermaine 94, 97, 104, 122, 124, 145, 151, 161, 168

Eckersley, Dennis 48
Eckstein, David 140
Edmonds, Jim 140
Einhorn, Eddie 13, 23, 52, 75
Eisenhower, Dwight 134
Eisenrich, Jim 27
Ensberg, Morgan 150
Erstad, Darrin 123, 125, 130, 131
Escobar, Kelvim 119, 129
ESPN 1, 82, 98, 108, 110, 175, 178
Evans, Dwight 40
Everett, Adam 146, 149, 156, 159, 161, 166

Everett, Carl 82, 83, 93, 98, 107, 110, 125, 145, 146, 149

Farmer, Ed 83, 103
Faust, Nancy 31, 32
Fehr, Donald 55
Fernandez, Alex 93
Fick, Robert 99
Fields, Josh 174
Figgens, Shone 129
Finley, Charlie 191
Finley, Steve 124, 125
Fisk, Carlton 13, 14, 20, 22, 22, 53, 93
Flanagen, Mike 18
Flannery, Tim 9
Fletcher, Scott 16, 27, 34, 39
Folding Chair 158
Folke, Keith 62, 69, 70, 72, 74, 77
Ford, Dan 21
Ford, Whitey 30, 117
Fox, Nelson 136
Franco, Julio 54, 93

Gallas, Rob 57
García, Freddy 104, 113, 125, 131
Gardenhire, Ron 85, 104
Garfien, Chuck 155, 181
Garland, Jon 93, 97, 98, 131, 157, 181
Garner, Phil 151, 158, 169
Gehrig, Lou 30
Gibson, Kirk 41
Glover, Gary 171
"Gods of Old Comiskey" 36
Gonzales, Mark 96, 148
Gooden, Dwight 138
Gorson, Tom 83
Gossage, Richard "Goose" 39, 111
Graffinino, Tony 109, 110, 111, 112, 114
"Green Monster" 113, 115
Griffey, Ken, Jr. 171
Grifol, Pedro 180
Guillén, Carlos 75
Guillén, Ozzie 11, 27, 29, 34, 45, 46, 49, 59, 62, 85, 87, 87–91, 91, 96, 98, 102, 103, 108, 112, 114, 115, 116, 130, 144, 148, 155, 157, 161, 171, 176, 178, 180, 181, 182, 183
Gutteridge, Don 190
Gwynn, Tony 54

Hahn, Rick 183, 184
Hairston, Jerry 168
Harrelson, Ken 41, 70, 102
Harris, Willie 98, 99, 161, 162

204

Index

Hawkins, Andy 28, 29, 30
Heaton, Neal 45
Hemond, Roland 51, 189–196
Henderson, Rickey 73, 75
Hermanson, Dustin 94
Hernandez, Keith 138
Hernández, Michel 175
Hernández, Orlando 114, 115
Hernández, Roberto 41, 42, 48, 62, 113
Hibbard, Greg 28
Hoiles, Chris 40
Holtzman, Ken 7
Horlen, Joe 40
Hough, Charlie 35, 93
Houston Astrodome 137, 141
Howry, Bobby 69, 70, 103
Hoyle, James 168
Hoyt, LaMarr 16, 17, 19, 48, 87

Iguchi, Tadahito 95, 98, 101, 110, 116, 151, 157, 166, 181

Jackson, Bo 27, 43–51
Jackson, Joe 116
Jackson, Reggie 190
Jauss, Bill 66
Jenkins, Bruce 96
Jenks, Bobby 94, 105, 111, 116, 148, 153, 155, 161, 162, 166, 172
Jiménez, D'Angelo 82
John, Tommy 51, 92
Johnson, Lance 27, 40
Johnson, Randy 101
Jones, Barry 30

Kansas City A's 31
Kata, Matt 169
Kelly, Pat 190
Kelly, Tom 85
Kerstain, Kevin 87
"Kids Can Play" 67
Kittle, Ron 2, 14, 18, 19
Kluszewski, Ted 74, 106
Knepper, Bob 138
Knight, Ray 139
Konerko, Paul 65, 68, 74, 75, 97, 98, 101, 102, 103, 107, 108, 113, 122, 124, 131, 132, 144, 152, 153, 164, 176, 177
Kopech, Michael 183
Kotchman, Casey 131
Koufax, Sandy 135
Kulpa, Ron 125

Lackey, John 122
Lamb, Mike 145, 146
Landrum, Tito 8, 22
Lane, Jason 153, 157
LaRussa, Tony 21, 23, 140, 178, 180, 184
Law, Rudy 21, 22
Law, Vance 8, 21
Lee, Carlos 65, 68, 74, 84, 94
Leyritz, Jim 30
Lidge, Brad 139, 140, 154, 161
Loazia, Esteban 83, 84
Logan, John 57
Lollar, Sherm 135
Lollar, Tim 87
Long, Bill 87
Lopez, Al 135
Lowenstein, John 19
Luzinski, Greg 13, 14, 15, 16, 17, 53
Lyle, Sparky 194

Mabry, John 139
Macías, José 139
Manrique, Fred 39
Mantle, Mickey 30, 137, 144
Manuel, Jerry 67, 68, 84, 144
Maris, Roger 30, 144
Marsh, Randy 130
Marte, Damaso 114, 158
Martínez, Edgar 73
Martinez, Tippy 21, 22, 23
Mauch, Gene 11
Mauer, Joe 171
May, Carlos 91
Mays, Joe 104
McCarthy, Brandon 104
McCarty, David 104
McCarver, Tim 119, 153, 154
McClelland, Tim 172
McCovey, Willie 41
McCuddy's Bar 37
McDowell, Jack 36, 47, 48, 58, 60, 202, 194
McGraw, Tommy 6
McGwire, Mark 27, 63
McKinney, Rich 192
McLemore, Mark 75
Melton, Bill 24, 51, 52
Mercedes, Yermin 184
Merrill, Stump 29
Milligen, Randy 40
Minute Maid Park 57, 139, 141, 157
Mobouquette, Bill 24
Molina, Bengie 125, 131
Moncada, Yoan 103
Montreal Expos 54

205

Index

Moore, Mike 44
Morrissey, Rick, 84–85, 103
Mueller, Bill 107, 110, 111
Murray, Eddie 18, 19
Myers, Chris 154

Neal, Charlie 135
Nelson, Jeff 151
Niekro, Joe 138
Nixon, Trot 108. 111, 114
Norton, Greg 63, 68

Oliva, Tony 109
Ordóñez, Magglio 64, 69, 72, 82, 84, 93
Orelud, John 74, 75, 109, 112, 114
Ortiz, David 107, 113
Orwell, George 9
Oswalt, Roy 141, 144, 156, 157
Ozuna, Pablo 98, 119

Paciorek, Tom 8, 14
Padilla, Doug 178
Palmer, Dean 68
Palmiero, Orlando 161
Paniagua, José 83
Pappu, Sridhar 66
Parque, Jim 68, 73
Pasqua, Dan 27, 28, 30, 41, 45, 88
Patterson, Danny 69
Paul, Josh 74, 119, 120
Pecota, Bill 42
Pelty, Barney 28
Perata, Jhonny 97
Perry, Gerald 27
Peters, Gary 5
Pettitte, Andy 12, 70, 150, 144, 155
Phillips, Paul 104
Phillips, Tony 93
Pierre, Juan 10
Pierzynski, A.J. 84–85, 95, 99, 107, 108, 109, 114, 115, 119–120, 125, 126, 130, 146, 149, 150, 151, 157
Pinella, Lou 74
Podsednik, Scott 94, 98, 108, 110, 122, 126, 149, 154, 155, 174
Polanco, Placido 105
Pujols, Albert 140

Qualls, Chad 152

Rader, Doug 15
Radinsky, Scott 36
Radke, Brad 83
Raines, Tim 35, 49 83, 93

Ramírez, Alexei 171, 175
Ramirez, Manny 107, 111, 113, 114, 172
Reagan, Ronald 58
Reardon, Jeff 33, 34
Reinsdorf, Jerry, 13, 26, 52, 55, 62, 66, 75, 81, 90, 164, 185, 186
Reneteria, Edgar 112, 113, 116
Reuschel, Rick 44
Reyes, Anthony 166
Reynolds, Harold 32
Richard, Kevin 137
Ripken, Cal, Jr. 19, 20, 39
Rivera, Juan 109
Roberts, Leon 16
Robinson, Brooks 147
Rodriguez, Alex 73
Rodríguez, Francisco 130, 131
Rodriguez, John 139
Rodríguez, Wandy 146
Roenicki, Gary 22
Roeper, Richard 41
Rogers, Phil 11, 85, 90
Romano, John 135
Rooney, John 66
Rosenberg, Bob 29
Rowand, Aaron 11, 97, 98, 101, 107, 109, 110, 111, 130, 131, 145, 150, 151, 165, 181, 182, 188
Ruth, Babe 30
Ryan, Nolan 138

Saberhagen, Bret 41
Salazar, Luis 87
Santanna, Ervin 124
Santo, Ron 24
Schneider, Herm 43
Scioscia, Mike 119, 129, 130
Scott, Mike, 138
Seinfield 57
Selig, Bud 55, 57
Sharma, Dr. 57
Short, Ed 190
Shelby, John 22
Sheridan, Pat 16
Siebern, Norm 31
Simas, Bill 69
Simmons, Todd 87
Singleton, Chris 69
Sirotka, Mike 76–78
Sizemore, Grady 12, 105
Smith, Al 115
Smith, Dave 139
Smith, Willie 7
Sotomayor, Sonia 58

206

Index

Sosa, Sammy 29, 33, 39, 46, 63, 64, 65, 168
South Side Hitmen 32
Soviet Union 134
SoxFest 1, 76, 81, 98, 181, 195
Span, Denard 71, 172
Speizio, Ed 194
Splittorff, Paul 15, 16, 17
Springer, Russ 148
Squires, Mike 21
Stanky, Eddie 6, 24. 25, 97
Stegman, Dave 16
Stewart, Dave 27, 28, 31
Stewart, D.L. 58, 59
Stone, Larry 96
Strawberry, Darryl 138, 139
Sturtze, Tanyon 69
Sutcliffe, Rick 9
Suzuki, Ichiro 176

Tanner, Chuck 190, 191
Taveras, Willie 146, 149, 151
Thigpen, Bobby 33
Thomas, Frank 33, 35, 39, 41, 46, 47, 48, 49, 54, 56, 58, 61, 63, 68, 72, 79, 80, 82, 88, 90, 98. 144
Thome, Jim 165, 166, 168, 172, 182
Timlin, Mike 115
Torberg, Jeff 34
Torre, Joe 82
Turang, Brian 44

Uribe, Juan 108, 110, 112, 113, 115, 146, 151, 154, 171
U.S. Cellular Park 82, 99, 143

Valentín, José 64, 70, 73, 82
Valentine, Fred 6
Valle, Dave 49
Varitek, Jason 108, 111, 114
Vázquez, Ramón 102
Veeck, Bill 4, 13, 26, 32, 52, 134, 135, 136, 202

Ventura, Robin 29, 35, 36, 39, 46, 48, 58, 61, 63, 92, 147, 183
Vizcaíno, José 154

Walker, Greg 14
Walsh, Ed 28
Walthan, John 27
Ward, Duane 46, 49
Warren, Mike 8, 18
Washington, U.L. 16
Weaver, Jeff 68
Wells, David 76–78, 110, 182
Werth, Jason 99
WGN-TV 40
Wheeler, Dan .151
"White Flag Trade" 61, 67, 75, 81
Whitesoxinteractive.com 11
Wickers, Ronny 81
Widger, Chris 101
Williams, Kenny 76, 77, 82, 93, 95, 163, 181, 185, 195
Williams, Matt 54
Williams, Ted 41
"Winning Ugly" 15, 17, 23, 33 46, 48
Wise, DeWayne 174, 175
WMVP-AM 78
Wood, Kerry 11, 80, 81, 85
Wood, Wilbur 51, 52, 80, 81, 192, 194
World Series Game Two Grand Slam 153
World Series Game Two Walk Off Home Run 155
World Series Game Three Winning Home Run 158
Wrigley Field 10, 24, 35, 64, 65, 81, 82, 79, 183
Wunsch, Kelly 75
Wynn, Early 75, 106, 136

Yastrzemski, Carl 25
Yellon, Al 96
Young, Delmon 171

www.ingramcontent.com/pod-product-compliance
Ingram Content Group UK Ltd.
Pitfield, Milton Keynes, MK11 3LW, UK
UKHW042003140426
5217IPUK00015B/959